CONTENTS

Marrakech Area by Area

Streetsmart

D0008807

Within each Top 10 list in this book, no hierarchy of quality or popularity is implied. All 10 are, in the editor's opinion, of roughly equal merit.

Front cover and spine Medersa Ben Youssef
Back cover Jemaa el Fna
Title page A decorated Moroccan door at Chez Ali restaurant, Marrakech

...nformation in this DK Eyewitness Top ...avel Guide is checked regularly. ... effort has been made to ensure that ...ok is as up-to-date as possible at the ... going to press. Some details, ...ever, such as telephone numbers, opening hours, prices, gallery hanging arrangements and travel information are liable to change. The publishers cannot accept responsibility for any consequences arising from the use of this book, nor for any material on third party websites, and cannot guarantee that any website address in this book will be a suitable source of travel information. We value the views and suggestions of our readers very highly. Please write to: Publisher, DK Eyewitness Travel Guides, Dorling Kindersley, 80 Strand, London WC2R 0RL, Great Britain, or email travelguides@dk.com

Welcome to
Marrakech

An age-old trading post, Marrakech is easily accessible from Europe. The city has an almost mythical quality, its pink ramparts dramatically backed by the purple peaks of the Atlas Mountains, while the spiced air of labyrinthine alleys lends an aura of magic and mystery. With Eyewitness Top 10 Marrakech, this vibrant city is yours to explore.

At the heart of the medieval walled Medina is **Jemaa el Fna**, a vast plaza filled with mesmerizing sights, from musicians and acrobats to fragrant street food stalls. It is the ideal spot from which to start exploring. To the south is the **Kasbah**, an area rich with palaces and tombs; to the north are the bustling **souks**, where almost anything can be bought, from herbal remedies to kaftans and carpets.

Outside the fortified gates, the **New City** districts of Guéliz and Hivernage offer orange-tree-lined avenues with a wealth of chic dining, drinking and shopping spots as well as cultural experiences. One of the area's unexpected delights is discovering the lush and colourful gardens, notably the **Majorelle** and **Agdal Gardens**.

Marrakech makes a splendid base for exploring southern Morocco. Hop on a bus or hire a car to experience the blue-and-white charms of the Atlantic port of **Essaouira**. Alternatively, head south to the **mountains** and to the **desert** beyond for imposing tribal fortresses, oasis villages, dune seas and a centre of international cinema.

Whether you are visiting for a weekend or a week, our Top 10 guide brings together the best of everything Marrakech has to offer. It gives you tips throughout, from navigating the souks to choosing a hammam, as well as eight easy-to-follow itineraries. With inspiring photography and detailed maps, this is the essential pocket-sized travel companion. **Enjoy the book, and enjoy Marrakech.**

Clockwise from top: **Jemaa el Fna, Riad Kniza, the port at Essaouira, Kasbah Aït Benhaddou, tile detail at Medersa Ben Youssef, a Marrakech carpet souk, camels at Merzouga oasis**

Exploring Marrakech

Marrakech may be low on museums and monuments, but a visit here is all about soaking up the atmosphere and culture. Even so, there are a handful of places that should not be missed. Four days allows you to see the best of the city and gives you time to make a day trip south into the mountains.

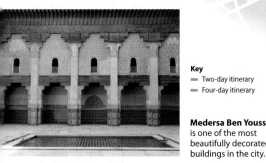

Key

━━ Two-day itinerary
━━ Four-day itinerary

Medersa Ben Youssef is one of the most beautifully decorated buildings in the city.

Two Days in Marrakech

Day ❶
MORNING
Start at **Jemaa el Fna** *(see pp12–13)*, then head to the **Saadian Tombs** *(see pp26–7)*. Have a leisurely lunch at **Café Clock** *(see p71)*.

AFTERNOON
Head over to the **Badii Palace** *(see pp30–31)*, then return to Jemaa el Fna by one of the rue Riad El Zitouns. Take a *calèche* tour of the **City Walls and Gates** *(see pp24–5)*, hopping out at **La Mamounia Hotel** *(see pp34–5)* for an early evening drink. Dine at the **Night Market** *(see pp14–15)*.

Day ❷
MORNING
From Jemaa el Fna, dive into the **souks** *(see pp16–17)*, then find your way to **Atay Café** *(see p77)* for lunch.

AFTERNOON
Head to the nearby **Medersa Ben Youssef** *(see pp28–9)*, then walk on to place du Moukef and catch a taxi to the **Majorelle Gardens** *(see pp32–3)*. Admire the exotic plants, then take a taxi to Guéliz for early evening drinks at the **Sky Bar** *(see p56)* before dining locally at **Al Fassia** *(see p83)*.

Four Days in Marrakech

Day ❶
MORNING
Start with a walk around the **Koutoubia** *(see pp20–21)*, before meandering over to the **Saadian Tombs** *(see pp26–7)*. Have lunch at **Café Clock** *(see p71)*.

AFTERNOON
Head over to the **Badii Palace** *(see pp30–31)*, then go by way of one of the rue Riad El Zitouns to **Jemaa el Fna** *(see pp12–13)*. Take a *calèche* tour of the **City Walls and Gates** *(see pp24–5)*, hopping out at **La Mamounia Hotel** *(see pp34–5)* for a pre-dinner drink. Travel back to Jemaa el Fna to dine at the **Night Market** *(see pp14–15)*.

The souks are a warren of passageways filled with brightly coloured local wares and intriguing sights and smells.

The Majorelle Gardens make for a peaceful getaway from the rush of the Medina.

Day ❷
MORNING
Head out from Jemaa el Fna and wander among the **souks** (see pp16–17) before finding your way to **Atay Café** (see p77) for lunch.
AFTERNOON
Visit the nearby **Medersa Ben Youssef** (see pp28–9) and wander the **Maison de la Photographie** (see p41). Make your way over to the Mouassine area, taking in **Dar Cherifa** (see p72), and dine at **Dar Moha** or **La Maison Arabe** (see p77; reservations required).

Day ❸
MORNING
Take a taxi to the **Majorelle Gardens** and the neighbouring **Musée Yves Saint Laurent** (see pp32–3) and

then another to Guéliz to lunch at **Kechmara** (see p83) and explore the local boutiques.
AFTERNOON
Return to the Medina for a leisurely afternoon at a hammam (see pp46–7). Head to Guéliz for a drink at the **Grand Café de la Poste** (see p83).

Day ❹
MORNING
Return to the Kasbah area to visit the impressive-looking **Bahia Palace** or the **Dar Si Said** Museum (see p68), then wrap up any souvenir shopping.
AFTERNOON
Take a taxi to the **Beldi Country Club** (see p53) for a late lunch, then spend the afternoon chilling beside the pool. Dine at **Comptoir Darna** (see p83).

Top 10 Marrakech Highlights

Minaret of the Koutoubia Mosque

TOP 10 Marrakech Highlights

Marrakech may only be Morocco's third most important city after Rabat and Casablanca, but its fabulous palaces and palm groves exercise a powerful hold over tourists. Once a market town, located on the edge of nowhere, it remains an exotic port of call.

① Jemaa el Fna
This is a vast plaza at the heart of the Medina (the old walled city). The site of parades and executions in the past, it is the centre of modern city life *(see pp12–13)*.

② The Night Market
By night, Jemaa el Fna turns into a circus, theatre and restaurant, with itinerant musicians and entertainers drawing crowds *(see pp14–15)*.

③ The Souks
Laid out in the narrow streets north of Jemaa el Fna is an array of souks. Different areas specialize in their own wares, selling everything from carpets and slippers to ingredients for magic spells *(see pp16–17)*.

④ Koutoubia Mosque

Marrakech's landmark monument has a tower that dominates the skyline for miles. It is closed to non-Muslims but it is an impressive sight none-theless *(see pp20–21)*.

⑤ City Walls and Gates
Marrakech's Medina is surrounded by several miles of reddish-pink dried-mud walls, punctuated by nearly 20 gates. Having proved ineffective against attackers throughout history, the walls are clearly more ornamental than functional these days *(see pp24–5)*.

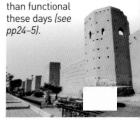

6 Saadian Tombs

A tranquil garden at the end of a narrow passageway shelters the royal tombs of one of Morocco's ruling dynasties. They were shrouded from the world until the 1920s (see pp26–7).

7 Medersa Ben Youssef

Behind a typically blank façade lies what is arguably the city's finest building. This ancient religious school features exquisite decoration (see pp28–9).

8 Badii Palace

The ruins of this once fabled palace provide a picturesque setting for nesting storks, and a salutary warning from history against extravagance (see pp30–31).

9 Majorelle Gardens

Jacques Majorelle, a French artist who came to Marrakech to recuperate, created this beautiful garden. It was later owned by French couturier Yves Saint-Laurent and is now open to the public (see pp32–3).

10 La Mamounia Hotel

With luxurious suites and exquisite surrounding gardens, La Mamounia is a *grande dame* among hotels, and has welcomed the visiting rich and famous for almost a century (see pp34–5).

TOP 10 ⭐ Jemaa el Fna

The Medina's central square means "Assembly of the Dead", a reference to a time when the heads of executed criminals would be displayed here on spikes. Although nothing so gruesome is on view today, the square is still populated with some extraordinary sights, including snake charmers, acrobats and colourfully costumed water sellers. Despite efforts to sanitize Jemaa el Fna with neat paving and ornamental barrows, the place remains endearingly chaotic.

1 Orange Juice Stalls
Sellers of freshly squeezed orange juice, with brightly painted barrows **(below)** are the first to appear on the square every morning.

2 Porters
With cars banned from crossing Jemaa el Fna, access to many of the hotels in the surrounding alleys is provided by the ubiquitous porter *(carroser)*, who carries travellers' luggage on a wheelbarrow to their riad, guesthouse or hotel in return for a small tip.

3 Calèches
Hop into one of the waiting *calèches* or horse-drawn carriages **(below)** parked along the square's west side. For a fee (visitors may need to bargain down from the original price), the *calèche* driver will do a circuit of the city walls. This experience is a favourite with children.

4 Acrobats
Acrobats and athletic young men **(left)** perform spectacular feats to entertain the audience and earn a few coins. Their repertoire usually includes cartwheels, somersaults and tottering pyramids.

5 Herbalists
These stand as testimony to the Moroccan belief in natural remedies. Compounds of ground roots, dried herbs and even desiccated animal parts are used for everything from curing colds to warding off the evil eye.

6 Tooth Pullers
These so-called "dentists" sit behind wooden trays filled with loose dentures ready to aid cash-poor locals with aching teeth.

NEED TO KNOW

MAP J3 ■ Medina

Café de France: 0524 44 23 19; open 7am–11pm daily (closes late in the summer); two restaurants; credit cards are not accepted

Calèche rides: place Foucauld, off Jemaa el Fna; prices vary, and tours can cost up to 110 Dh for 15 to 20 minutes.

■ In addition to Café de France there are many other cafés with terraces offering prime seating overlooking the square, including Chez Chegrouni (see p71).

AN UNPLANNED MASTERPIECE

Jemaa el Fna square is considered to be a "Masterpiece of the Oral and Intangible Heritage of Humanity" by UNESCO. This is an international list that includes pieces of culture such as song cycles, theatrical traditions and sacred spaces. Inclusion in the list is intended to raise awareness and preserve something unique and irreplaceable; Jemaa el Fna certainly qualifies.

⑩ Water Sellers
Known by the locals as *gerrab*, the traditional water sellers roam the square in colourful costumes and tassel-fringed hats, ringing copper bells to announce their arrival **(left)**. The brass cups are exclusively for Muslims, while the white-metal cups are for everyone else. The water may upset visitors' stomachs.

⑦ Fortune-Tellers
Throughout the day, impossibly wrinkled elderly women squat beneath umbrellas with packs of tarot cards to read the fortunes of passersby.

⑧ Café de France
There are several good places to sit and watch the incessant entertainment of the square over a coffee, but the raffish air of the Café de France **(right)** lends it an added appeal, making it a favourite with tourists and locals alike.

⑨ Snake Charmers
Spot snake charmers weaving their way through the market stalls. Some will try to put the reptile around your neck and then charge you for the privilege, so it is best to steer clear.

TOP 10 ⭐ The Night Market

Each evening as the sun goes down, dozens of open-air kitchens are set up on the east side of Jemaa el Fna. Serving areas are erected and tables and benches are put out to create one vast al fresco eatery. Beneath a hanging cloud of smoke created by the crackling charcoal grills, locals and visitors alike tuck into a vast array of Moroccan cuisine. Nearly every stall has its own speciality, from snails in spicy broth and chunks of lamb stuffed into sandwiches, to chicken pastillas and humble hard-boiled eggs.

1 Le Grand Balcon du Café Glacier
One of the best places to observe the spectacle of the Night Market is the rooftop terrace of Le Grand Balcon du Café Glacier. Visit at sunset for superb views.

2 Cross-dressing Dancers
These are men who dance wildly while dressed in women's clothing. It's an age-old practice and one that lends a surreal quality to the atmosphere of the square at night.

4 Promenade
Once dusk begins to fall, many visitors take a leisurely stroll through the square and along Rue Bab Agnaou.

5 Musicians
A smattering of musicians and groups of Gnawa **(below)** specialize in hypnotic rhythms and enchanting melodies which set the crowds swaying. Entranced listeners can linger in the square long after everyone else has gone home.

The Night Market on Jemaa el Fna

3 Shopping
Walk around to view what's on offer and when you see something you like, take a seat and just point to what you want. Prices are usually posted and everything is fairly inexpensive.

6 Storytellers
Gifted orators enthral their rapt audience with tales of Islamic heroes and buffoons. Sessions end on a cliffhanger – the outcome is only revealed the following night.

7 Street Food
The ingredients arrive fresh at the market each evening and the food is cooked from scratch in front of you. Plates and utensils are often washed in water that isn't changed for much of the night, so it is best to get your food served on paper and eat with your fingers.

⑧ Local flavours

Some of the most popular food offerings are the varieties of *brochette* – grilled lamb and chicken – along with bowls of soup, spicy merguez sausages, grilled fish and bowls of boiled chickpeas. Those feeling adventurous can try the stewed snails.

THE GNAWA

The Gnawa came to Morocco as slaves from sub-Saharan Africa. Over the centuries they have kept their culture alive through oral traditions, particularly music. Played on simple string instruments known as *gimbri*, their music is looping and repetitive, intended to induce an almost trance-like state in the dancers and the vocalists who often sing and chant along with the musicians. Gnawa music has made a great impact on the global music scene.

⑨ Entertainers

Excited onlookers surround a menagerie of tricksters, sundry wild-eyed performers and fortune-tellers. This is where the Moroccan belief in everyday magic is on full display. And it is not put on for tourists.

⑩ Henna Painting

Day or night, ladies with piping bags full of henna paste paint hands and feet with the most intricate of designs **(above)**. Be aware that an illegal colouring substance that can cause severe skin problems is sometimes used, so approach with caution.

NEED TO KNOW

MAP J3 ■ The Night Market sets up at sunset daily and runs until around midnight or later in the summer months.

Le Grand Balcon du Café Glacier: 0524 44 21 93; open 6am–10:30pm daily

■ Although Marrakech has a very low crime rate, the crowds milling around Jemaa el Fna at night are perfect cover for pickpockets. Be careful with handbags, wallets and purchases.

■ If you find the food stalls at the Night Market to be intimidating, you can always opt for the relative familiarity of salads, pizza and pasta at Le Marrakchi restaurant *(see p71)* instead.

TOP 10 ⭐ **The Souks**

Marrakech's earliest inhabitants made their living from trade, bartering with the Africans, and the Spaniards who came by sea. Luxuries like gold and ivory came from the south, while leather, metalwork and ceramics were sent north. Even today, trade continues to be the city's mainstay, with thousands of craftsmen making a living among the maze of souks that fill much of the northern half of the Medina. A trip to the souks is part history lesson, part endurance trial – testing how long travellers can keep their purse in their bag or their wallet in their pocket.

1 Souk des Tapis
Once used to auction slaves, this souk is now crowded with carpet sellers **(right)**.

2 Fondouks
The *fondouk* is an ancient hostelry for travelling merchants, built around a courtyard. These days, most are gritty workshops.

3 Rahba Kedima
This open square is home to sellers of dried scorpions and leeches as well as other bizarre substances and objects for use in traditional black magic **(above)**.

4 Souk El Kebir
Found straight on from rue Semmarine, this is the heart of the souks – a narrow alley that lurches from side to side and up and down. It is lined by tiny shops each overflowing with goods, especially leather.

5 Souk El Bab Salaam
This covered market serves the nearby Mellah quarter with everything from food to caged birds.

6 Souk des Teinturiers
Sheaves of freshly dyed wool are hung from ropes strung across one particular alleyway of the dyers' souk for a vibrant, colourful scene.

7 Souk Cherifia
A small three-storey mini-market within the souks, this is the place for edgier finds among a plethora of quirky, designer-owned boutiques *(see p76)*.

The Souks

8 Souk des Ferronniers

The sound of hammering fills the air in this medieval part of the Medina where ironworkers (above) create furniture, lanterns and other items.

9 Rue Semmarine

The main route into the souks is via an arch just north of Jemaa el Fna and along this perpetually busy sun-dappled alley. Shop owners along Semmarine attempt to entice visitors with a miscellany of robes, kaftans, carpets and antiques.

10 Souk des Babouches

Every shop and stall here sells nothing but brightly coloured, soft-leather, pointy-toed slippers known as *babouches* (left). Prices can vary widely between around 60 Dh and 400 Dh.

NEED TO KNOW

MAP K2 ■ Medina ■ Many of the shops and stalls in the souks are closed on Fridays

■ You will get lost in the souks. Alleys are narrow, winding and constantly branching, while landmarks are few. However, the area covered is small and you are never more than a few minutes' walk back to Jemaa el Fna. Watch out for the constant stream of scooters and bicycles in the narrow lanes.

■ Café Arabe, near the Souk des Teinturiers, and Café des Epices in the Rahba Kedima are both great places for some respite from the bustle (see p77).

The Guide Issue

A guide to the souks is really not necessary. Although the souks are a warren, the area is not too large and it's never hard to find your way back to some familiar landmark. Any "best places" your guide may lead you to are often only the best because they offer your guide the highest commission.

Marrakech Souvenirs

Colourful Moroccan pottery featuring traditional patterns and glazes

1 Pottery

Each region of Morocco produces its own distinctive pottery. The Marrakech style is plain terracotta finished with colourful glazes, and ceramics from the Akkal factory would not look out of place in a cutting-edge design shop. Visit the big pottery souk outside Bab Ghemat, found to the southeast of the Medina, for a wide variety.

2 Carpets

Marrakech is famed for its carpets, made by the tribes of the south who each have their own patterns. Some carpets are very old and are made of genuine cactus silk, but these are rare. Most sold today, though beautiful, are quite modern and made from non-natural fibres. Beware the salesmen's patter: buy a carpet if you like it, not because you have been told it is a good investment.

3 Candles

Candles are used to great effect in local riads, bars and restaurants.

They are sold in all shapes, sizes and colours (and frequently scents), and some of the designs are highly inventive. You can find them in the souks and Guéliz boutiques, although the greatest selection is probably to be found in the industrial quarter outlets of Sidi Ghanem (see p52).

4 Lanterns

There are two types of lanterns: those that hang from the ceiling and those that sit on the floor. The former (known as *fanous*) are typically metal and come in elaborate shapes with intricate decoration. The latter are made of skin and goats' hair and are usually very colourful. Look for them in the northern part of the souk or head down to the place des Ferblantiers.

Lantern

5 Marra-Kitsch

A trend among local designers involves taking Marrakech iconography and giving it a Pop Art twist. Hassan Hajjaj, known as the "Andy Warhol of Marrakech", makes *fanous* (lanterns) from sheets of tin printed with advertising logos.

6 Babouches

Babouches are Moroccan slippers, handmade from local leather, although increasingly the *babouches* found in the souks are made of a synthetic plastic that only looks like leather. In their most basic form they are pointy-toed and come in a variety of colours but are otherwise plain. It is becoming popular for boutiques and shops to customize their *babouches* with a silk trim, or even carve the leather with exquisite designs.

7 Jewellery

The local Berber jewellery is silver, chunky and heavy. However, a number of artisans in Marrakech, both local and foreign, produce more modern designs. Look out for designer Joanna Bristow's brilliant creations in select hotel boutiques such as La Mamounia *(see pp34–5)*.

A selection of Moroccan jewellery

8 Fashion

Marrakech has inspired countless foreign couturiers – from Yves Saint-Laurent to Tom Ford. But the city has a vibrant fashion scene of its own, spearheaded by local designers including Artsi Ifrach, Norya Ayron and Noureddine Amir. Check out Souk Cherifia and other boutiques in Mouassine *(see p76)*, and, in the New City, visit the excellent concept store 33 rue Majorelle *(see p82)*.

An array of leather bags

9 Leather Bags

Marrakech is known for its leather. The animal hides are treated by hand in the tanneries *(see p74)* in the east of the Medina, and then dyed and shaped. Unsurprisingly, the shops of the souk are filled with leather goods, from purses and handbags to book bindings. Do plenty of window shopping before settling on an item.

10 Argan Oil

Argan oil is an almost mystical substance to which all kinds of properties are attributed *(see p95)*. Part of its mystique can be credited to the rarity of argan trees, which only grow in southwest Morocco. The oil is sold all over the souks but much of it is low grade. To ensure you are buying quality oil, it is best to visit a reputable dealer.

Extracting argan oil

TOP 10 ⭐ Koutoubia Mosque

Its minaret is the city's pre-eminent monument, towering above all else, and has always been the first visible sign of Marrakech for travellers approaching from afar. Its iconic status is fitting as the mosque is not only the city's main place of worship, but also one of its oldest buildings – it was built back in the 12th century, not long after Marrakech was founded. The designer of the Koutoubia minaret went on to create Tour Hassan in the Moroccan capital, Rabat, and the tower of the Giralda in Seville. As with nearly all mosques and shrines in Morocco, non-Muslims are not permitted to enter; however, the architecture can be appreciated from outside.

4 The Mosque Plan

The mosque's plan is rectangular in shape. The plain main entrance to the east leads to a vast prayer hall with eight bays and horseshoe arches. North of the prayer hall is a 45-m (148-ft) wide courtyard with an ablution fountain and trees.

6 Minaret

The purpose of a minaret is to provide a high platform from which the muezzin can make the call to prayer five times a day. Rather than a simple staircase, the Koutoubia's towering minaret **(right)** has a spiralling ramp wide enough for a horse to be ridden to the top.

1 Koubba Lalla Zohra

This white tomb **(above)** houses the body of Lalla Zohra, a slave's daughter said to have transformed into a dove each night.

2 Mosque of the Booksellers

The Koutoubia was built in 1158. Its name means the *Mosque of the Booksellers*, which is a reference to a small market that once existed in the neighbourhood where worshippers could buy religious texts.

5 Dar El Hajar

Two wells on the piazza allow visitors to view the buried remains of the Dar El Hajar (House of Stone), a fortress built by the Almoravids. It was destroyed when the Almohads captured the city in 1147 *(see p38)*.

7 Prayer Times

Exact times of daily prayer change with the seasons, but they are observed five times a day, with sessions held pre-dawn, noon, late afternoon, sunset and late evening, as indicated by the muezzin, who sings the call to prayer. The most important prayers of the week are those on Friday at noon.

3 The Minaret Decoration

Originally the whole minaret was encased in tiles and stucco, but now only two bands of blue ceramic remain **(right)**.

⑧ Ruins of the Almohad Mosque

Next to the Koutoubia are the remains of an earlier mosque, built c 1147. The bases of the prayer hall's columns, secured behind railings, are clearly visible (below). They were revealed during excavations by Moroccan archaeologists.

⑨ Koutoubia Gardens

South of the mosque is a garden with a mix of palms and deciduous trees, topiary hedges and colourful roses (above).

HEIGHTS OF GOOD TASTE

The Koutoubia minaret's continued dominion over the skyline is owed to an enlightened piece of legislation imposed by the city's former French colonial rulers. They decreed that no building in the Medina should rise above the height of a palm tree, and that no building in the New City should rise above the height of the Koutoubia's minaret. The ruling still holds today. Only Muslims are allowed to enjoy the view from the top of this building.

NEED TO KNOW

MAP H4 ■ Avenue Bab Jedid, Medina

Mosque: open only during prayer times; closed to all non-Muslims

Gardens: entry is free to both Muslims and non-Muslims

■ Although access is denied to non-Muslims, one of the doors on the east wall is often open so visitors can peer through for a view of the prayer hall and its seemingly endless arcades of horseshoe arches.

■ Café Kif Kif can be found across the road from the Koutoubia and has a terrace with great views of the mosque.

⑩ Tomb of Youssef Ben Tachfine

Just north of the mosque, glimpsed through a locked gate, is a walled area containing the dilapidated mausoleum of Youssef Ben Tachfine (1009–1106), tribal leader of the Almoravids and the man credited with the founding of Marrakech.

TOP 10 ⭐ City Walls and Gates

The city walls date from the 1120s when, under threat of attack from the Almohads of the south, the ruling Almoravid sultan, Ali Ben Youssef, decided to encircle his garrison town with fortifications. The walls he had built were up to 9 m (30 ft) high and formed a circuit of 10 km (6 miles), with some 200 towers and 20 gates. Even today, the walls remain largely unchanged.

NEED TO KNOW

Medina

Bab Debbagh: permission required to access the roof (not always open to visitors)

Calèche tours: Place Foucault, off Jemaa el Fna; prices vary, but rides can cost around 110 Dh for 15 to 20 minutes.

■ Walking a circuit around the walls can be unpleasant in the heat. It is better to visit the gates individually or take a *calèche* tour.

■ If you take a *calèche* ride around the walls, make sure that you carry bottled water, as it can get hot and dusty.

2 Bab Berrima

Apart from serving as perimeter defences, walls and gates were also used to divide up the interior of the Medina. For instance, a wall separated the royal kasbah quarter from the city – Bab Berrima was one of the gates between these two distinct zones. This gate leads to the Medina's main souks.

3 Bab er Robb

This was the original southern city gate. The gatehouse building is now occupied by a pottery shop and all foot and car traffic passes through a modern breach in the old walls. The name translates as "Lord's Gate".

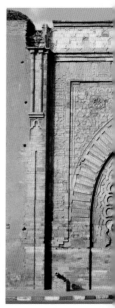

1 Pisé

The walls are built from a mixture of mud, straw and lime (known as pisé), which becomes as hard as brick on drying. The distinctive pinkish-red hue (above) is a result of pigments in the earth.

City Walls and Gates

Previous pages Elaborate zellij tiling at the Dar Si Said Museum

6 Place des 7 Saints

Just outside the north side of the walls stand seven stone towers, each topped by a tree **(left)**. This giant ensemble pays homage to the seven patron saints of Marrakech *(see p75)*.

THE RED CITY

Marrakech's distinctive colouring comes from pigments in the local soil mixed to make the *pisé* from which the city's buildings were traditionally constructed. In the last century, this was threatened by new building materials such as concrete. The ruling French decreed that all new buildings be painted pink – a rule that continues to be enforced today with pleasing aesthetic results.

8 Bab Agnaou

The most beautiful of the city's gates, the "Gate of the Gnawa" is the only stone-built one **(left)**. It was erected during Almohad sultan Yacoub El Mansour's reign in the 12th century.

9 Bab Debbagh

This gate gives access to the tanneries, and when it is open, visitors can ascend an internal staircase to the gatehouse roof for sweeping city views.

4 Bab Doukkala

This massive gate, built by the Almoravids in the 12th century, now stands isolated from the walls thanks to 20th-century urban planning. The cavernous interior of the rooms make them perfect for occasional use as an event space.

7 Bab El Khemis

The northernmost gate, this is the most decorative, with a semicircle of stalactite mouldings arcing over the entrance. A lively flea market is held here on Thursdays from 8am to midday.

10 Dar El Haoura

West of the Agdal Gardens, this curious freestanding fortress used to be a garrison for cavalry and its horse ramp is intact to this day.

Calèche Tours 5

The best way to view the walls is by a *calèche (see p12)*. You can take a complete circuit for a reasonable price **(right)**.

TOP 10 ⭐ Saadian Tombs

This is the secluded burial place of a dynasty noted by novelist Edith Wharton for its "barbarous customs but sensuous refinements". The 66 royal tombs that are housed here date from the late 16th and early 17th centuries, but were unknown to the outside world until the 1920s when they were revealed by the curiosity of a French official. The complex may be modest in size but it is beautifully decorated in the Alhambran style with plenty of carved cedar, stucco and multi-coloured tiling. The tombs have three main burial chambers arranged around a small garden.

1 Hall of Twelve Columns

This chamber holds the tombs of the Sultan Ahmed El Mansour and his entire family **(below)**. The stele is in finely worked cedar wood and stucco. The graves are beautifully designed and made from Italian Carrara marble.

2 Morning Market

A small square formed by the convergence of several narrow side streets south of the tombs plays host to a modest fruit and vegetable market (every morning except Fridays).

3 Prayer Hall

The first chamber, intended as a place of prayer, now contains tombs. Most of these date back to the era of the Alaouite rulers.

5 Kasbah Mosque

Pre-dating the tombs by around 400 years, this well-known mosque was originally built in 1190. Since then it has undergone a number of renovations. However, the cut-brick on green-tile background that decorates the minaret is the original **(below)**.

4 Rue de la Kasbah

When you exit the tombs, take a left to reach this main street, cutting through the old kasbah quarter. It runs arrow-straight down towards the Grand Méchouar.

6 ETS Bouchaib

One of two government-run stores selling fine local handicrafts, this is a one-stop opportunity to purchase kaftans, jewellery, carpets and ceramics. With everything at a fixed price, it is ideal for anyone who dislikes haggling in the souk. Items can be expensive but are of good quality.

8 Entranceway

Reached via narrow, twisting passageways (above), the tombs remained a closely guarded secret for centuries. Even today, a visit to the complex retains an element of discovery for tourists.

9 Saadian Dynasty (1549–1668)

Setting out from their powerbase in Taroudant, to the south of the Atlas Mountains, the Saadians defeated the ruling Merenids of Fès. Having established their court at Marrakech, they revitalized the city and endowed it with grand monuments. They were in power for nearly 120 years until the Alaouites came to power.

7 Main Chamber

A grand pavilion (above) at the garden's centre is the only real bit of architecture in the complex. A tall, green-tiled, roofed structure in the Andalusian style, it has three soaring portals with beautifully carved wood and a stucco frieze of eight-pointed stars. Housed within are more mosaic-covered tombs, including that of Mohammed ech-Cheikh, founder of the Saadians.

ISLAMIC BURIALS

In Islam, it is customary to begin the burial process within 24 hours of death. After a ritual washing, the body of the deceased is wrapped in a funeral shroud. It is then put directly into the ground, laid on its right side and facing Mecca. Graves are raised to prevent anyone from sitting or walking on them. Islam forbids cremation.

10 The Garden

This serene garden (below) has countless headstones dotted among the bushes and scrubby plants. These mark the tombs of several children, as well as guards and servants. The garden is hugely popular with the local stray cats.

NEED TO KNOW
MAP J6

Saadian Tombs: rue de la Kasbah, Medina; open 9am–noon, 2:30–6pm daily; adm 10 Dh

ETS Bouchaib: 7 derb Baissi Kasbah, off rue de la Kasbah; 0524 38 18 53; open 9:30am–8pm daily; MC, V accepted

■ This is a very small site, easily crowded by the presence of just a single tour group. Visit early morning or late afternoon for the best chance of avoiding the crush.

■ La Sultana Hotel (see p112) next door has a good rooftop terrace restaurant open to non-guests.

🔟⭐ Medersa Ben Youssef

While not the oldest or most significant of Marrakech's monuments, the *medersa* is one of the city's most impressive buildings, and it allows entry to non-Muslims. Founded in the 14th century, it was restored and enlarged by the Saadian sultan Moulay Abdellah in around 1565. All the fine decorative detailing that characterizes the golden age of Moroccan architecture is evident in the *medersa*. The building has also had a brush with movie stardom as an Algerian Sufi retreat in the movie *Hideous Kinky*.

Main Courtyard

At the heart of the *medersa* is a light-filled courtyard with arcades down two sides, a rectangular pool in the middle and a prayer hall. Every surface has some decoration **(right)**.

2 Dar Bellarj

To the north of the *medersa's* entrance, Dar Bellarj is a former stork hospital (the name means "House of the Storks"). The building now houses a beautiful cultural centre with a programme of regularly changing exhibitions.

4 Chrob ou Chouf Fountain

A little north of the *medersa*, this handsome fountain is worth seeking out. With a big cedar lintel covered in calligraphy, it is from a time when it was a pious act to provide a public source of clean drinking water. Its name means "drink and look".

3 Student Cells

Arranged on two levels around the central courtyard are 130 tiny rooms, much like monks' cells **(above)**. Nearly 900 Muslim students studied here until the *medersa* fell out of use in the 1960s.

NEED TO KNOW

MAP K2 ■ Medersa Ben Youssef, Medina ■ 0524 44 18 93 ■ www.medersa-ben-youssef.com

Open 9am–5pm daily; Adm: 20 Dh

Nearby, you can also visit the **Musée de Marrakech**. ■ www.museede marrakech.ma

Open 9am–6pm daily (except religious holidays); Adm: 10 Dh; combined ticket to visit the Musée de Marrakech and Koubba El Badiyin (when it reopens after renovations, *see pp74–5*) 60 Dh

■ Musée de Marrakech has a courtyard that is used as an exhibition space.

6 Carved Stucco

The panels of intricately carved plaster that stretch above the tiling are decorated with inscriptions or geometric patterns **(left)** – depiction of humans or animals is prohibited by Islam.

BEN YOUSSEF MOSQUE

The *medersa*, in its earlier days, was part of the complex of the nearby Almoravid mosque, which was founded by Ali Ben Youssef during his reign (1106–42). For several centuries, this was the focal point of worship in the Medina, and, together with the *medersa*, it was considered a significant centre of the Islamic religion in Morocco.

8 Tiling

The lowest part of the courtyard wall is covered with *zellij* (glazed tiles) in an eight-pointed star motif **(below)**. Above this is a band of stylized Koranic text, interwoven with floral designs.

5 Prayer Hall

The elaborate prayer hall has an octagonal wooden-domed roof supported by marble columns **(below)**. The stucco features rare palm motifs and some calligraphy of Koranic texts. The room is well lit by gypsum windows.

7 The Role of the Medersa

A *medersa* was once a place for religious instruction – a theological college. The students who boarded here would have studied the Koran and discussed it with the institute's *fqih* or imam (learned religious figures).

9 Rue du Souk des Fassis

This winding alley to the *medersa's* east is lined by beautifully restored *fondouks* and old hostels. One is now a restaurant, Le Foundouk.

10 Ablutions Basin

Enter via a long corridor that leads to a square vestibule. On the left is a marble basin carved with floral motifs in the Andalusian style.

TOP 10 ⭐ **Badii Palace**

It reputedly took armies of labourers and craftsmen 25 years to finish the Badii Palace. Completed in 1603, it was said to be among the most magnificent palaces ever constructed, with walls and ceilings encrusted with gold, and a pool with an island flanked by four sunken gardens. This grand folly survived for all of a century before yet another conquering sultan stripped the place bare – a process that took 12 years – and carted the riches to his new capital at Meknès. All that survives are the mudbrick ruins.

1 Mosque Minbar

An "annexe du palais" in the southeast corner displays the 12th-century pulpit *(minbar)* from Koutoubia Mosque. Intricately carved, this is a celebrated artwork of Moorish Spain.

2 Storks

The protrusions in the crumbling walls are well loved by the city storks that have made their nests here **(above)**. An old Berber belief has it that storks are actually transformed humans.

3 Khaysuran Pavilion

A pavilion on the north of the great court and once the palace harem, this space now serves as an exhibition hall, showing work by local and locally based foreign artists.

4 Rooftop Terrace

At the northeastern corner of the palace is the only intact tower with an internal staircase to the roof. At the top, it is possible to get a sense of the immense size of the complex **(above)**.

5 Basins and Gardens

The palace's central courtyard is dominated by five basins and four sunken gardens planted with orange trees **(below)**. The central basin has an island that comes alive every July for the Festival of Popular Arts. It is also used as a venue during the International Film Festival *(see p40)*.

6 Sultan Ahmed El Mansour

The palace was built by El Mansour who became sultan after the Battle of Three Kings (1578), when the Moroccans defeated the Portuguese. Great wealth was accrued from the ransom of Portuguese captives and the riches were poured into the palace.

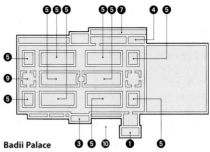

Badii Palace

7 The Gatehouse

The approach to the palace is found between twin high walls. On its completion, the gatehouse carried an inscription glorifying the palace. Now it is a ruin and the complex is entered through a breach in the crumbling walls.

8 A Sinister Omen

At a banquet to celebrate the palace's completion, a guest declared, "When it is demolished, it will make a fine ruin." The omen is now a reality.

9 Pavilion of 50 Columns

The ruins around the courtyard were probably summer houses. The Koubba El Khamsiniya **(left)** on the west side is named after the 50 pillars used to build it.

THE BATTLE OF THE THREE KINGS

In an attempt to steal the throne from his uncle, Abdel Malek, the Saadian sultan Abu Abdallah Mohammed II declared war along with King Sebastian of Portugal. All three died in the battle, fought in Ksar El Kebir, between Tangier and Fès. Malek was succeeded by his brother, Ahmed El Mansour, builder of the Badii Palace.

10 Underground Passages

Beside the annexe, a path leads down into the former stables and dungeon **(below)**. Though you can still enter, the chambers are only partially lit.

NEED TO KNOW

MAP K5 ■ Place des Ferblantiers, Medina

Open 9am–5pm daily

Adm: 10 Dh; plus 10 Dh for the *minbar* pavilion

■ It is a big site with little shelter, so avoid visiting in the heat of the afternoon.

It is a good idea to bring bottled water.

■ In summer it is a venue for the Marrakech du Rire comedy festival.

■ Kosybar (*see p71*) is place des Ferblantiers' rooftop terrace. It offers the perfect spot for a bird's-eye view of the palace walls.

TOP10 ⭐ Majorelle Gardens

These are the most famous of Marrakech's numerous gardens (see pp50–51), and the legacy of an expatriate French painter, Jacques Majorelle, who considered himself a "gardenist". In 1923, he acquired land and set about creating a botanical sanctuary around his studio. Majorelle opened his gardens to the public in 1947 and they remained popular until his death 15 years later. They fell into disrepair until 1980, when they were rescued by partners Yves Saint-Laurent and Pierre Bergé.

1 Bassins and Fountains

The garden has a fountain and two large *bassins*, or pools (above), the smaller of which is fed by a sloping channel. Next to the museum, a third pool is filled with a school of golden carp.

2 Boutique

In the northeast corner, a small boutique sells an interesting selection of quality local handicrafts including clothing, jewellery and miscellaneous leather products such as bags, sandals and beautifully bound notebooks. However, there is a notable paucity of information concerning Majorelle and his garden.

3 Majorelle Blue

The name Majorelle lives on in an electrifying shade of cobalt blue – known as "Majorelle blue" – that is widely used in the garden (above).

4 Majorelle's Paintings

The museum's first room has a series of lithographs depicting various Atlas kasbahs. Some of Majorelle's most acclaimed works were the tourism posters that he created for Morocco.

5 Yves Saint-Laurent Memorial

The designer, who died in 2008, is remembered by a Roman column, which came from his Tangier home, placed on a red-ochre base (left). His ashes were scattered around the gardens.

YVES SAINT-LAURENT

French designer Yves Saint-Laurent first visited the city in 1962. By the end of the 1960s, he had bought his first house here. Later, he moved into a villa next to Majorelle Gardens, which he purchased and saved from being turned into an apartment complex. After his death a small memorial column was placed in the gardens. The Musée Yves Saint Laurent opened in late 2017, just weeks after the death of Pierre Bergé.

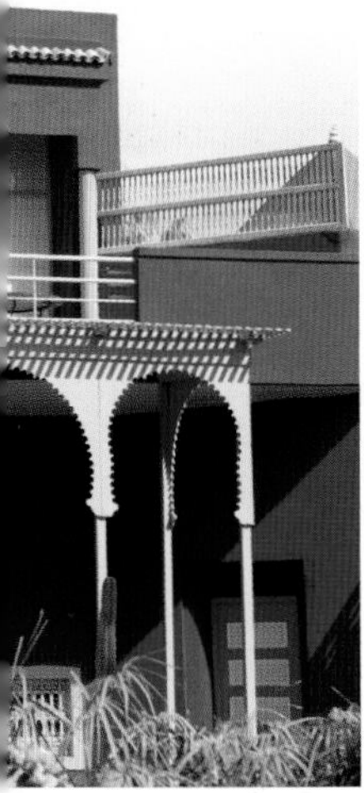

7 Berber Museum

Jacques Majorelle's garden-villa-studio is now a museum dedicated to the indigenous Berber people. More than 600 items illustrate aspects of their traditional culture **(above)**.

8 Galerie Love

The "LOVE" posters Yves Saint-Laurent created using collage and sent yearly as New Year's greetings to friends and clients are exhibited here.

6 Jacques Majorelle

French artist Jacques Majorelle (1886–1962) came to Morocco in 1917 to recuperate from his heart problems and immediately saw the painterly potential of southern Morocco.

9 Musée Yves Saint Laurent

Situated next door to the Majorelle Gardens, this modern museum displays some of the French couturier's best-known looks. There is also an arts centre and an auditorium.

10 The Plants

A beautiful bamboo "forest" and an arid cactus garden with species from around the world share the garden **(above)**. Most stunning of all are the flowering masses of red and purple bougainvillea.

NEED TO KNOW

MAP C4 ■ Rue Yves Saint-Laurent, Guéliz ■ 0524 31 30 47 ■ www.jardin majorelle.com

Open Oct–Apr: 8am–5:30pm daily; May–Sep: 8am–6pm daily; Ramadan: 9am–5pm daily

Adm to gardens: 70 Dh; Berber Museum: 30 Dh

Musée Yves Saint Laurent Marrakech: 0524 29 86 86; open 10am–6pm Thu–Tue; Adm 100 Dh; www.museeyslmarrakech.com

■ **This is another very small site that is easily crowded by just a single tour group. Visit early in the morning or late in the afternoon for the best chance of avoiding the inevitable crowds and long queues.**

TOP 10 ⭐ La Mamounia Hotel

One of the world's great old hotels, La Mamounia has been welcoming the rich and famous since opening its doors in 1923, with Winston Churchill one of its most celebrated guests. Originally built as a palace in the 19th century for the crown prince of Morocco, it was turned into a hotel for the Moroccan railways by the French. Set within 7 hectares (17 acres) of delightful gardens, it is surrounded by the city's 12th-century red ochre ramparts.

1 The Rooms
Many of the rooms in this landmark hotel have been luxuriously renovated using wood and leather in warm Moroccan shades.

NEED TO KNOW

MAP H5 ▪ Avenue Bab Jedid, Medina ▪ 0524 38 86 00 ▪ www. mamounia.com

The gardens: open 24 hours; non-guests allowed entry

▪ Non-guests wishing to visit La Mamounia should dress smartly – people wearing flip flops, shorts and T-shirts are generally not allowed to enter.

▪ The hotel boasts several restaurants and bars, but perhaps the most pleasurable of these is the lunchtime buffet that is served daily beside the swimming pool.

The main entrance to La Mamounia Hotel .

2 Churchill's Paintings
Churchill would paint in the afternoon and was fond of Marrakech's extraordinary light. A couple of his paintings still hang in the hotel.

3 Guestbook
Scribbles by Sean Connery, Catherine Deneuve, Bill Clinton, Kate Winslet and Will Smith – La Mamounia's *livre d'or* must be among the starriest guestbooks.

4 The Man Who Knew Too Much
Several scenes of this 1956 Alfred Hitchcock thriller (**left**) featuring James Stewart and Doris Day were shot in the hotel, as well as other locations across the city.

The Suites ⑤
The most famous of the hotel's several grand suites is the one named after Winston Churchill **(right)**. The decoration is intended to evoke the politician's era and the suite contains several artifacts, including his pipe.

Winston Churchill ⑦
"This is a wonderful place, and the hotel one of the best I have ever used," were the words Churchill used in a letter to his wife, Clementine, to describe the hotel and the city that he adored. Churchill famously invited Franklin Roosevelt here during World War II *(see p43)*.

Churchill Bar ⑩
One part of the hotel that was not altered during the recent makeover was this bar, named after the hotel's most famous guest. Cigar smoking is permitted, but shorts and T-shirts are not allowed.

The Architects ⑧
The original architects of La Mamounia blended Art Deco with traditional Moroccan motifs. In 1986, renovations were carried out by the designers of Morocco's royal palaces, further changing the character of the building.

The Gardens ⑥
The acres of formal European-style gardens were laid out for the prince and predate the construction of the hotel. Well-manicured paths lead between ponds and flowerbeds to a central pavilion **(right)**.

Majorelle Ceiling ⑨
Winston Churchill met fellow painter Jacques Majorelle in the winter of 1946 during one of his many stays at La Mamounia. The politician persuaded the hotel's management to commission a mural by Majorelle **(left)**, which you can now see on the ceiling of the extended lobby. Today, the Frenchman is best known for his creative masterpiece, the Majorelle Gardens *(see pp32–3)*.

The Top 10
of Everything

The serene, elaborately designed
inner courtyard of Riad Kniza

Moments in History

1 Founding of Marrakech

The Almoravids, the most powerful Berber tribe, founded the military outpost of Marra Kouch in 1062, giving them control of the Saharan trade routes.

Koutoubia Mosque, Marrakech

2 The Almohads Take Marrakech

The Almohads lay siege to Marrakech in 1147 and the city changed hands. Their impressive monuments, including the Koutoubia Mosque, still dominate Marrakech.

Sultan Moulay Hassan

3 Decline Under the Merenids

Emerging from eastern Morocco, the Merenids took the city from the weakening Almohads in 1269. During their rule, Marrakech was sidelined and reduced to a provincial outpost after they chose the northerly city of Fès as their power base.

4 The Saadians Return the Throne to Marrakech

Prosperity returned to Marrakech under the Saadians, who overthrew the Merenids in 1549. This first Arab dynasty expanded their territory across the Western Sahara and over to Mali and Mauritania.

5 Moulay Ismail

The Saadians were swept aside by the Alaouites in 1668. Their second ruler, Moulay Ismail, was noted as much for his cruelty as for his diplomacy skills. He reigned for 55 years. The Alaouite dynasty still rules Morocco today.

6 The Sultan of Spliff

Moulay Hassan, a powerful sultan who ruled from 1873 to 1894, legalised cannabis cultivation. Today the Rif region is one of the world's largest cultivators, even though several measures have been taken to try to eradicate this.

7 Imposition of French Rule

The lynching of Europeans in Casablanca gave France an excuse to implement her territorial ambitions. The consequent March 1912 Treaty of Fès made Morocco France's protectorate. In this period, a whole *nouvelle ville* (new city) was built outside the walls of the Medina.

8 The Lord of the Atlas

The French enlisted tribal warlord Thami El Glaoui to rule southern Morocco from 1918 to 1955. The self-styled "Lord of the Atlas" was known for his cruelty and ruled the city with an iron fist.

Tribal warlord Thami El Glaoui

9 The Crowning of the King

November 1955 marked the return of exiled Sultan Mohammed V who was crowned king, with Morocco gaining independence a year later. The current ruling monarch, Mohammed VI, is his grandson.

10 Marrakech Goes Global

It is claimed that a French TV programme in the 1990s, stating that a palace in Marrakech could be bought for the price of a flat in Paris, was the catalyst for the city's new-found popularity. Five-star hotels and budget airlines soon followed suit.

TOP 10 MARRAKECH READS

Author Peter Mayne

1 A Year in Marrakech (1953)
Peter Mayne's engaging journal captures the essence of a city little-changed since medieval times.

2 Cinnamon City (2005)
The true story of the purchase and renovation of a dilapidated Marrakech riad by Briton Miranda Innes.

3 The Last Storytellers: Tales from the Heart of Morocco (2011)
BBC journalist Richard Hamilton relates tales heard from the professional storytellers from Jemaa el Fna.

4 In Morocco (1920)
A visit to Morocco and Marrakech in 1917 inspired novelist Edith Wharton to try her hand at travel writing.

5 Morocco That Was (1921)
An entertaining account (especially of the Moroccan royalty) by *Times* correspondent Walter Harris.

6 Welcome to Paradise (2003)
Mahi Binebine tells the story of would-be migrants to Europe, setting off from a café on Jemaa el Fna.

7 Lords of the Atlas (1966)
A history of the colourful El Glaoui era by Gavin Maxwell.

8 Hideous Kinky (1998)
Esther Freud's autobiographical account of a dysfunctional 1970s childhood in Marrakech.

9 The Tangier Diaries (1997)
An account by John Hopkins of 1950s Tangier, featuring drug-fuelled forays to Marrakech.

10 Marrakech: The Red City (2003)
A collection of writings on Marrakech down the ages from writers such as George Orwell and Edith Wharton.

🔟 Arts and Culture

Modern art at David Bloch Gallery

1 David Bloch Gallery

MAP B5 ▪ 8 bis rue des Vieux Marrakchis, Guéliz ▪ 0524 45 75 95 ▪ Open 3:30–7:30pm Mon, 10:30am–1:30pm and 3:30–7:30pm Tue–Sat ▪ www.davidblochgallery.com

To see the new face of Marrakech art, visit this stylish gallery specializing in contemporary Moroccan art and graffiti.

2 Musée Douiria de Mouassine

MAP J2 ▪ 4–5 derb el Hammam, Mouassine ▪ 0524 38 57 21 ▪ Open 10am–6pm Sat–Thu ▪ Adm ▪ www.museedemouassine.com

This former home of a 16th-century Saadian noble is one of Marrakech's most delightful museums, with the family's living quarters carefully restored. There are great views from the small rooftop café (see p74).

3 Musée d'Art et de Culture de Marrakech (MACMA)

MAP C5 ▪ 61 rue de Yougoslavie, Guéliz ▪ 0524 44 73 79 ▪ Open 10am–7pm Mon–Sat ▪ www.museemacma.com

Opened in 2016, this elegant gallery displays works by artists who fell in love with Marrakech including Jacques Majorelle, Eugène Delacroix and Raoul Dufy. Temporary exhibitions highlight Moroccan artists.

4 Galerie 127

MAP B5 ▪ 127 ave Mohammed V, Guéliz ▪ 0524 43 26 67 ▪ Open 3–7pm Tue–Sat ▪ www.galerie127.com

The first gallery in North Africa devoted to photography, this white-walled space in Guéliz exhibits many big names.

5 Marrakech International Film Festival

Sponsored by movie fan King Mohammed VI, the festival was launched in 2001 and is held in December. A number of stars have graced the red carpet, including Martin Scorsese and Sean Connery.

6 Dar Cherifa

This 16th-century town house is a cultural centre that hosts regular exhibitions, with Gnawa musicians (see p15) often performing on opening nights. The small library offers art and heritage books to browse while enjoying tea or coffee (see p72).

Marrakech Biennale performance

7 Marrakech Biennale

www.marrakechbiennale.org

Occurring in even-numbered years, the Biennale focuses on cutting-edge contemporary visual art, literature and film, making great use of a variety of eclectic venues.

Maison de la Photographie

8 Maison de la Photographie

MAP K2 ■ 46 rue Souk Ahal Fassi, Medina ■ 0524 38 57 21
■ Open 9:30am–7pm daily
■ www.maisondelaphotographie.ma

This is a small museum dedicated to photographs taken by travellers to Morocco from the late 19th century to the 1960s. It occupies a beautiful old courtyard house not far from the Medersa Ben Youssef. The rooftop café is a refreshing place to stop for a glass of mint tea and take in the view.

9 Galerie Rê

MAP C5 ■ Résidence El Andalous III, cnr rue de la Mosquée & rue Ibn Toumert, Guéliz ■ 0524 43 22 58
■ Open 10am–1pm, 3–8pm Mon–Sat
■ www.galeriere.com

This is a contemporary art gallery at the northern end of the New City. Here, visitors can enjoy regularly changing exhibitions.

10 Marrakech National Festival of Popular Arts

Troupes from all over Morocco perform at this celebration of Berber music and dance held every year in June or July. Don't miss the magnificent *fantasia*, an energetic charge of Berber horsemen outside the ramparts near the Bab El Jedid.

TOP 10 MOROCCAN CULTURAL FIGURES

1 Tahar Ben Jelloun
Morocco's best-known French-based writer won the French Prix Goncourt in 1987 for his novel *The Sacred Night*.

2 Mahi Binebine
This Marrakech-based artist authored the excellent *Welcome to Paradise*.

3 Hassan Haggag
The graphic artist behind the T-shirts worn by the staff at London's famous Moroccan restaurant, Momo.

4 Laïla Marrakchi
This Casablanca-born film-maker's debut feature, *Marock,* caused a scandal on its release in 2006.

5 Farid Belkahia
Famous for painting on lamb-skin canvases, Belkahia, one of Morocco's most influential artists, died in 2014.

6 Jamel Debbouze
Known for his roles in *Amélie* and *Days of Glory*, this French-Moroccan actor also runs the Marrakech du Rire comedy festival.

7 Elie Mouyal
This well-known architect is hugely popular among celebrities looking for a suitably fancy residence.

8 Master Musicians of Jajouka
International fame came upon this musical ensemble from a north Moroccan village, courtesy of the Rolling Stones.

9 Leila Abouzeid
The first female Moroccan author to have her work translated into English.

10 Hassan Hakmoun
Based in New York, this Moroccan trance specialist performed on Jemaa el Fna as a child.

Hassan Hakmoun

📟10 Celebrity Visitors

French designer Yves Saint-Laurent

1 Yves Saint-Laurent
The French couturier first visited the Red City in 1962, a trip that reignited memories of his childhood in Oran, Algeria. He returned a few years later and bought a house. The city soon found its way into his work, with the colours and patterns of southern Morocco influencing his collections. He spent part of every year here in a villa adjacent to the Majorelle Gardens *(see pp32–3)*.

2 George Orwell
The author of *Animal Farm* and *Nineteen Eighty-Four* was in Marrakech in 1939 on the advice of his doctor after being diagnosed with tuberculosis. While here, he wrote *Coming Up for Air* and an essay, *Marrakech*.

George Orwell

3 The Rolling Stones
Brian Jones of the Rolling Stones visited Marrakech in 1966 and brought the rest of the band on the next trip. They stayed at the Hotel Es Saadi in Hivernage, where Cecil Beaton photographed Mick Jagger and Keith Richards by the pool.

4 Poppy Delevingne
Where fashion designers go, models follow. Kate Moss was famously photographed here in 1993 and, in 2014, Poppy Delevingne hosted a wedding celebration in the city with friends including Alexa Chung, Georgia May Jagger and Sienna Miller. Marrakech is very much the A-list party venue of choice – a boho alternative to Ibiza.

John Paul Getty Jr and his wife

5 John Paul Getty Jr
In the 1960s, American oil heir John Paul Getty Jr and his wife Talitha owned a place in the Medina. They were photographed by Patrick Lichfield clad in kaftans on their mansion's roof terrace with a backdrop of the Atlas Mountains.

6 Paul Bowles
The author of *The Sheltering Sky* was an occasional visitor to Marrakech. In 1961, Beat poet Allen Ginsberg took an iconic photograph of Bowles on the roof terrace of Le Grand Balcon du Café Glacier.

David Beckham

In May 2015, David Beckham celebrated his 40th birthday with a bash at the Amanjena hotel, a secluded luxury resort just outside Marrakech. It was attended by a number of his celebrity friends, including Tom Cruise, Eva Longoria, Gordon Ramsay and the Spice Girls.

Charles de Gaulle, second from right

⑧ General Charles de Gaulle

After the Casablanca Conference (a meeting of leaders of the Allied forces) in January 1943, General Charles de Gaulle travelled to Marrakech, staying at La Mamounia Hotel. The hotel's director had to create a bed for him in order to accommodate his considerable frame.

⑨ Robert Plant

Led Zeppelin vocalist Robert Plant and guitarist Jimmy Page first visited Marrakech in 1975. Twenty years later, they recorded some video footage in Jemaa el Fna to accompany the release of their album "No Quarter".

⑩ Winston Churchill

Between 1935 and 1959, British Prime Minister Winston Churchill visited Marrakech no fewer than six times. "Here in these spacious palm groves rising from the desert," he reportedly said, "the traveller can be sure of perennial sunshine." He spent his time at La Mamounia Hotel (see pp34–5) writing his memoirs and painting.

TOP 10 MOROCCO FILMS

1 Othello (1951)
Orson Welles put the Moor in Morocco, shooting much of his famously troubled masterpiece in Essaouira.

2 Mission Impossible: Rogue Nation (2015)
Morocco was the star of this globe-trotting action movie, with scenes filmed at Jemaa el Fna as well as in Casablanca and Rabat.

3 Our Man in Marrakesh (1966)
The city of Marrakech features heavily in this little-seen silly spy comedy.

4 Kundun (1997)
The Atlas Mountains were cast as Tibet in Scorsese's epic. Props can still be seen at Kasbah du Toubkal (see p63).

5 Hideous Kinky (1998)
The souks and Jemaa el Fna were prominent in this film adaptation of Esther Freud's autobiographical book.

6 Gladiator (2000)
Russell Crowe is sold into slavery at Aït Benhaddou (see p100). Also shot here were The Last Temptation of Christ and Lawrence of Arabia.

7 Sex and the City 2 (2010)
Marrakech, which doubled as Abu Dhabi, was the only thing that came out of this farrago with any credit.

8 Alexander (2004)
Alexander of Macedonia was, in fact, Alexander of Marrakech.

9 Babel (2006)
The village of Tazatine in southern Morocco appears in this film.

10 The Man Who Knew Too Much (1956)
Alfred Hitchcock filmed actors James Stewart and Doris Day in La Mamounia and Jemaa el Fna.

The Man Who Knew Too Much (1956)

Moroccan Architecture

1 Stucco Plaster
A decorative element of Moroccan architecture, carved plaster can cover entire walls in fantastic design. The work is executed by craftsmen while the plaster is still damp – the patterns are sketched onto the surface, then gouged out with hammer and chisel.

2 Pigeonholes
The numerous pigeonholes peppering the walls in the city are, in reality, remnants of wooden scaffolding used to erect walls.

3 Tadelakt Plaster
This technique was initially used in bathhouses to counter the heat and moisture. Walls are treated with a limestone plaster, which, once set, is polished with flat stones, then glazed with egg whites and polished again with local black soap made from olives. The finished surface looks akin to soft leather.

4 Courtyards
A distinctive feature of Islamic architecture is its focus on the interior rather than the exterior, which is generally windowless. Courtyards serve as air-wells into which the cool night air sinks. They also allow women to enjoy the outdoors without having to cover up.

Typical Moroccan courtyard

Carved woodwork on a door

5 Carved Woodwork
Although some of the same designs are used to decorate both plaster and wood, the latter often has inscriptions in Arabic, the sacred language in which the Koran was revealed to the Prophet Mohammed. The inscriptions are of a religious nature and invariably praise the glory of Allah. They are both decorative and informative.

6 Fountains
Fountains and basins are required for ritual ablutions before prayers. With such an arid climate, the provision of drinking water is also seen as a charitable act.

7 Square Minarets

The square design of Moroccan minarets can be traced to the Umayyad rulers of Islamic Spain, who were of Syrian origin. Syrians are almost unique in the Middle East for their square minarets, probably influenced by the church towers built by Syrian Christians.

8 Pisé

The basic building material used in Morocco, *pisé* is wet earth that is mixed with straw and gravel pounded between two parallel boards and strengthened by lime. If it is not made well, the mixture can cause the structure to crumble in the rain – southern Morocco is littered with semi-melted buildings.

Colourful *zellij* terracotta tiles

9 Zellij Tiling

One of the most striking features of Moroccan architecture is its use of small, multicoloured tiles laid in complex geometric patterns. This is known as the *zellij* technique, where tiles are created as large squares and then hand-cut into smaller shapes. Conventional shapes and sizes are typically used, though there are as many as 360 different types of pieces.

10 Horseshoe Arches

Properly known as *outrepassé* arches, these are where the arch curves back inwards after its widest point, to give an effect like a keyhole or horseshoe. This design is most commonly associated with Moorish Spain and North Africa.

TOP 10 HISTORIC BUILDINGS

Bab Agnaou gate

1 Bab Agnaou
This gate into the kasbah quarter is an impressive keyhole arch *(see p25)*.

2 Koutoubia Mosque
Marrakech's biggest and tallest minaret *(see pp20–21)*.

3 Badii Palace
Its *pisé* walls are in an advanced state of dilapidation with clearly visible "pigeonholes" *(see pp30–31)*.

4 Bahia Palace
This 19th-century palace features a riot of *zellij* work *(see p68)*.

5 Medersa Ben Youssef
This structure displays an array of decorative elements, including fine *zellij* work, superbly carved stucco and woodwork *(see pp28–9)*.

6 Tin Mal Mosque
Some rare, surviving carved plasterwork dating to the early Almohad dynasty adorns the interiors of this mosque *(see p94)*.

7 Koubba El Badiyin
The earliest example of Islamic architecture in Marrakech with beautifully carved plasterwork seen nowhere else in Morocco *(see p75)*.

8 Dar Cherifa
Home to a busy cultural centre, this is an example of a wealthy courtyard with some extraordinary carved woodwork *(see p72)*.

9 Dar El Bacha
Enough dazzling, multicoloured, polychromically patterned *zellij* tiling to make your head spin.

10 Dar Si Said Museum
Visit this museum for an insight into architectural techniques and decoration *(see p68)*.

🔟 Hammams and Spas

1 Heritage Spa

MAP H2 ▪ 40 Arset Aouzal, Bab Doukkala, Medina ▪ 0524 38 43 33 ▪ Open 10am–8pm daily ▪ www.heritagespamarrakech.com ▪ Credit cards accepted

A modern spa with a wide variety of treatments and packages at reasonable prices, the Heritage is extremely friendly and has English-speaking staff. It is an ideal option if you have never experienced a *hammam* before.

Bottles used in spa treatments

2 Les Bains de Marrakech

MAP J6 ▪ 2 derb Sedra, Mechouar Bab Agnaou, Kasbah ▪ 0524 38 64 19 ▪ Open 9am–7pm daily ▪ www.lesbainsdemarrakech.com ▪ Credit cards accepted

This spa provides a dazzling selection of treatments such as water massage, shiatsu massage and the intriguingly named "four-handed massage". Unusually, the *hammam* offers small, mixed steam-bath cubicles (swimsuits are compulsory). The adjacent Riad Mehdi is there to quench your thirst after all the exertion.

Les Bains de Marrakech

3 Hammam Ziani

MAP K4 ▪ Rue Riad Zitoun el Jedid, Medina ▪ 0662 71 55 71 ▪ Open 9am–10pm daily

Located near the Bahia Palace, this *hammam* offers all the facilities that you would expect (scrub, soak, steam and pummel) in surroundings that are significantly cleaner than those found in other medina bathhouses.

4 Hammam de la Rose

MAP J2 ▪ 130 Dar El Bacha, Medina ▪ 0524 44 47 69 ▪ Open 10am–8pm daily ▪ www.hammamdelarose.com ▪ AmEx, MC, V accepted

Smarter than the public *hammams* but not as over the top as some full-service spas, the Rose is a good mid-range option for Moroccan-style luxury that doesn't break the bank. Reasonably priced packages include hammam treatments with body scrubs followed by massages.

5 La Maison Arabe

The *hammams* housed in larger riads and hotels are often restricted to guests, but not at La Maison Arabe *(see p112)*. Book yourself in for a vigorous *gommage* (rubdown) with a *kissa* (loofah mitten) and follow it up with a soothing back, face, or foot massage.

6 Hammam El Bacha

MAP H3 ▪ 20 rue Fatima Zohra, Medina ▪ Open: men 7am–1pm daily; women 1–9pm daily ▪ No credit cards

This is one of the city's most historic *hammams*; the staff of the Dar El Bacha, just across the road, were its first patrons. While it is still functioning, it is poorly maintained. The highlight is an impressive 6-m (20-foot) cupola in the steam room.

The opulent basement *hammam* at La Sultana hotel

7 La Sultana

A five-star hotel *(see p112)* next to the Saadian Tombs, La Sultana has a beautiful basement spa complete with a star-domed marble Jacuzzi, a *hammam*, a fitness centre, balneotherapy baths, open-air massage cabins as well as a solarium. Packages include massages, aromatherapy and seaweed treatments. It gets very busy so book well in advance.

8 Farnatchi Spa

The day spa in Riad Farnatchi *(see p112)* is exquisitely designed, with private marble *hammams* featuring vaulted ceilings and a charming courtyard café for lunch. Visitors can even hire the whole spa for the day. Combine a *hammam* body scrub treatment with an aromatic mask and finish with a beldi massage using black soap.

9 Royal Mansour

As ornate and opulent as the five-star hotel itself *(see p112)*, the Royal Mansour's spa makes a statement as soon as you enter. The exquisite white wrought-iron atrium brings to mind a giant bird enclosure – complete with the sound of birdsong. Sprawling across three floors, the spa also includes a large indoor swimming pool as well as a fitness centre.

10 Riad Noir d'Ivoire

This hip riad *(see p115)* includes Coco's Spa, offering a *hammam* and spa treatments such as an hour-long massage in front of a fire. Other treatments include hot-stone massages, reflexology and Coco's signature massage combining Moroccan and Thai methods.

Inner courtyard, Riad Noir D'Ivoire

🔟 Riads

Shaded dining areas and colourful cushions on the roof terrace at Riad Kniza

1 Riad Kniza

A 200-year-old town house that has been beautifully restored by a local antiques dealer, Riad Kniza showcases the best of Moroccan arts and crafts throughout its rooms and public spaces. Attentive service adds to the sensation that you're staying in a palace *(see p114)*.

2 Riad Kheirredine

Its blend of traditional Berber decor and 21st-century gadgetry – including the Bluetooth music systems – makes this riad stylish and smart. But what sets it apart is the exemplary service, including free bottles of mineral water and pastries, as well as prepaid mobile phones for its guests *(see p114)*.

3 Riad AnaYela

A captivating riad with a compelling story: the name ("I am Yela") comes from the first words of a manuscript that was found in a hidden room during the riad's reconstruction, telling a tale of forbidden love. Small and lavishly appointed, it offers a special stay *(see p114)*.

4 Riad Farnatchi

The intimate yet deluxe Farnatchi has a design that is a playful update of the local aesthetic. Luxurious suites feature sunken baths and stylish private terraces offering gorgeous panoramic views. Almost like mini-riads, some suites have marble fountains and elaborate fireplaces *(see p112)*.

Courtyard pool at Riad Farnatchi

5 Riad Noir d'Ivoire

This is a good option for fashionistas, with sumptuous photoshoot-friendly decor, a backlit bar serving a range of delicious cocktails, a relaxing *hammam* and its own boutique *(see p115)*.

6 Dar Attajmil

This tiny riad with four rooms and a roof terrace overlooks a small courtyard full of banana trees. The rooms have dark-wood ceilings and *tadelakt* bathrooms *(see p44)*. Its restaurant offers organic food from the owners' farm near Essaouira. The proprietors also run a two-bedroom mini-riad up the road and can easily arrange cookery classes and airport transfers *(see p114)*.

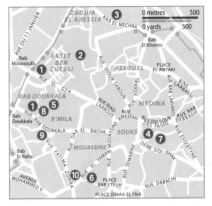

7 Tchaikana

Reasonably priced, this riad has two suites, two big double rooms and one smaller double room. The decor in each room is beautiful and highlights the "African" in North African. The rooms are set around a large central courtyard that is used for breakfasts and candlelit dinners. Don't miss the riad's celebrated crêpes at breakfast *(see p117)*.

8 Riad Al Massarah

While this Anglo-French-owned riad is run with an environmental and social conscience, there has been no skimping on the standard of its amenities, luxuries or the quality of its service *(see p114)*.

9 La Maison Arabe

More a small hotel than a riad, La Maison Arabe began life as a restaurant in the 1940s, closing in 1983 and reopening 16 years later. It feels almost like a country mansion and retains a definite colonial air. Guests can re-create Moroccan cuisine at one of the riad's renowned cookery workshops. There is a small garden pool on site, and a larger one just a 15-minute free shuttle ride away *(see p112)*.

La Maison Arabe restaurant

10 El Fenn

Founded by Vanessa Branson, El Fenn *(see p112)* is a sort of super-riad with its four courtyards, three pools, bar, restaurant, *hammam*, library, cinema screening room and collection of modern art including Branson's own work – all shared by just 28 rooms and 56 guests. The roof terrace offers spectacular views of the Atlas Mountains.

🔟 Parks and Gardens

Majorelle Gardens viewpoint

1 Majorelle Gardens
Formerly owned by Yves Saint-Laurent *(see p42)*, the gardens were first created by expatriate French artist Jacques Majorelle. Though small, they are quite lovely, with bamboo groves, cacti, palms, and pools floating with water lilies. The artist's former studio is now a mini Berber Museum, painted a searing blue that is known as "Majorelle blue" *(see pp32–3)*.

Menara Gardens pavilion

2 Mamounia Gardens
Landscaped with flowerbeds and olive and citrus groves, these gardens predate La Mamounia Hotel. The Arset El Mamoun were established in the 18th century by Prince Moulay Mamoun, laid out around a central pavilion that served as a royal residence *(see pp34–5)*.

3 Le Jardin Secret
MAP J2 ▪ 121 rue Mouassine, Medina ▪ 0524 39 00 40 ▪ Open Feb, Mar & Oct 9:30am–6:30pm daily; Apr–Sep 9:30am–7:30pm daily; Nov–Jan 9:30am–5:30pm daily ▪ Adm ▪ www.lejardinsecretmarrakech.com

Opened to the public in 2016, this large courtyard garden is in the middle of the Medina. Pleasant rather than spectacular, it is a fine place to relax with a mint tea.

4 Menara Gardens
MAP B7 ▪ Ave de la Menara, Hivernage ▪ 0524 43 95 80 ▪ Open 9am–5pm daily ▪ www.jardin-menara.com

Laid out in the 12th century, the Menara Gardens, with their orchard, pool and pavilion, epitomize a typical Islamic garden. The large pool is overlooked by a green-tile-roofed pavilion.

8 Jnane El Harti

Pretty and often quiet, this neatly planted green space is beloved by locals, with its proximity to places of work making it a favourite lunchtime hangout. Come evening, visitors will spot young couples looking for a few private moments away from the prying eyes of families and relatives (see p80).

9 Koutoubia Gardens

On the south side of the landmark mosque, these formal gardens have stone pathways lined with flowerbeds and topiary hedges. The roses seem impervious to the heat and appear to be in bloom throughout the year (see p21).

5 Musée de la Palmeraie

MAP F4 ■ Dar Tounsi, route de Fes ■ 0628 03 10 39 ■ Open 9am–6pm daily ■ www.musee-palmeraie.com

This harmonious blend of nature and culture is set in a vast palm oasis (the Palmeraie) on the edge of town. The museum's elegant galleries exhibit contemporary Moroccan art. There are also several fine thematic gardens inhabited by tortoises, turtles and frogs.

6 Agdal Gardens

MAP E7 ■ South of the Grand Méchouar ■ Open 7:30am–5pm Fri & Sun; closed if the king is in residence

Dating back to the 12th century, the Agdal comprises several linked gardens including an orange grove, an olive plantation, vineyards, and orchards of pomegranates and figs. There is a large pool at its heart the Tank of Health – in 1873, Sultan Mohammed IV tragically drowned in it when he went boating with his son. Beware of pickpockets.

7 Cyber Parc Arsat Moulay Abdeslem

MAP G3 ■ Ave Mohammed V ■ Open 7:30am–6:30pm daily

This public garden, between avenue Mohammed V and the walls of the Medina, has been given a makeover. The lawns, divided by palm-shaded pathways, are a favourite lunch spot. The park also has free Wi-Fi hot spots.

Dar al Hossoun gardens

10 Dar al Hossoun

Taroudant ■ 0665 02 82 74 ■ www.alhossoun.com

The desert gardens at Hossoun, a guesthouse in the town of Taroudant in southern Morocco, contain more than 900 different species of plants. The gardens can be booked for private tours.

Off the Beaten Track

① Jarjeer Donkey Sanctuary
MAP C1 ■ Rue d'Amizmiz
■ www.jarjeer.org

Jarjeer is a retirement home, care centre and orphanage for mules and donkeys in a beautiful valley in the foothills of the Atlas Mountains. There is a coffee shop here as well as donkey rides for children. It is 24 km (15 miles) from Marrakech on the Route d'Amizmiz, near Oumnass village.

② Sidi Ghanem
MAP C1 ■ 219 Quartier Industriel Sidi Ghanem

Anyone serious about shopping for homeware and interior decor items (candles, pottery, linen, furniture) should head to this industrial estate on the northern fringes of town, which has become the city's "design district". It is home to more than a dozen fantastic shops (start with Maison Fenyadi) and has a scattering of cafés and eateries for between-purchase sustenance.

Crockery at Maison Fenyadi

③ Horse Trekking
www.naturallymorocco.co.uk

An excellent way of getting off the beaten track is to head out of the city into the surrounding desert on horseback. There are plenty of companies in and around Marrakech that provide horses, equipment and guides. The length of rides available varies from a few hours to a whole week, and there are a number of treks on offer, including coastal, desert and mountain rides.

Miâara Jewish Cemetery

④ Miâara Jewish Cemetery
MAP L5 ■ Ave Taoulat El Miara

In the early 20th century there were 36,000 Jews living in Marrakech, but now there are only maybe a couple of hundred. Evidence of this lost populace can be seen at this immense, sprawling, 200-year-old walled cemetery in the little-visited southeast corner of the Medina.

⑤ La Pause
MAP C1 ■ Douar Lmih Laroussiene, Agafay ■ www.lapause-marrakech.com

Another option for getting out of the city, this lodge is set in the arid Agafay valley about 40 minutes southwest of Marrakech. It is a chic eco-resort offering a choice of accommodation – nomad tents strewn with Berber rugs and cushions, or partially open huts made of *pisé*. There are plenty of activities on offer, including swimming, horse trekking, *pétanque* and golf.

6 Take a Day Trip

Head out of Marrakech in any direction to lose the crowds immediately. There are a number of worthwhile day trips for which your hotel can organize a private car and driver. One of the least-visited places is the barrage at Lalla Takerkoust, where you can swim while enjoying superb mountain views *(see p63)*.

7 Marché Central

MAP C4 ■ Rue Ibn Toumert

Set away from the Medina, just east of place du 16 Novembre and behind the modern shopping centre, this is where locals and the city's expats do their shopping. Mixed in with the fruit, veg and miscellaneous food stalls are a handful of craft shops where both quality and price tend to be better than the souks.

8 Souk El Khemis

MAP D4 ■ Bab el Khemis

Entrepreneurs renovating riads scout this flea market just north of the Medina walls for unusual finds, including carved doors and other bits of recycled handiwork.

9 Palmeraie Palace

This palm grove north of the city is the favoured retreat of the rich. Among the secluded villas are also several upmarket hotels, including the Palmeraie – one of North Africa's leading golf resorts. Guests can play its 27-hole course and there are numerous restaurants and bars as well as a free kids' club *(see p117)*.

Beldi Country Club

10 Beldi Country Club

MAP C1 ■ Route de Barrage
■ www.beldicountryclub.com

Escape the dust and chaos of the Medina to this chic rural retreat just beyond the city centre. Among shaded olive groves and rose gardens are restaurants, pools, a tennis court and a spa. Visitors can book cooking and pottery lessons, and the site includes a luxurious hotel for overnight stays.

One of the pools at Palmeraie Palace

🔟 Children's Attractions

Local performers dressed in vibrant clothes at Jemaa el Fna

① Jemaa el Fna
With jugglers, acrobats and musicians, Jemaa el Fna will definitely capture children's imaginations. Make sure kids have adequate protection from the heat during the day, especially during the summer months when temperatures can top 40° C (104° F) *(see pp12–13)*.

② Horse Riding
Royal Club Equestre, Route du Barrage (opposite Oasiria) ■ 0524 38 18 49
Ponies and horses can be ridden at the Palmeraie Palace *(see p117)*. The Royal Club Equestre also has horses and ponies available to hire for both adults and children under ten years of age (rides of around 15 minutes each are offered).

③ Swimming
The Palmeraie Palace *(see p117)* allows non-guests the use of its swimming pool for a fee. It also has a popular children's play area.

④ Jnane El Harti
This public park has a small kids' play area with two concrete grey dinosaurs for them to clamber up and slide down. There is a McDonald's opposite *(see p80)*.

⑤ Child-Friendly Eating
Parents of fussy eaters might be glad of Le Catanzaro *(see p83)*, an Italian restaurant in Guéliz that makes mini pizzas from a wood-fired oven for children, as well as classic pasta dishes and generous desserts, including giant pavlovas. Alternatively, there are ubiquitous McDonald's outlets nearby for a quick bite.

⑥ Kawkab Jeux
MAP C5 ■ 1 rue Imam Shafi, Kawkab Centre, Hivernage ■ 0524 43 89 29 ■ Open 2–10pm Tue–Fri, 9:30am–11pm Sat, Sun and holidays ■ www.kawkab-jeux.com
South of the Jnane El Harti, next to the Royal Tennis Club, this bright coffee shop and ice-cream parlour also has an indoor and outdoor play area. Kids can play table football, table tennis and video games.

Kawkab Jeux play area

7 Tansift Garden
Circuit de la Palmeraie
- Open 8am–11:30pm daily

Off the main route through the Palmeraie among the palms is the Tansift Garden. This has a children's playground and is home to the Palmier d'Or café. Pony and camel rides are also available nearby.

8 Oasiria
Km 4, Route du Barrage ■ 0524 38 04 38 ■ Open 10am–6pm daily; closed late Oct–late Mar ■ Adm ■ www.oasiria.com

South of the city, this large waterpark features a wave pool, a covered and heated pool, an artificial river, beach and many restaurants. A free shuttle runs every 45 minutes from 9:30am from Jemaa el Fna and Guéliz.

Artificial river, Oasiria

9 Child-Friendly Accommodation
Coralia Club Palmariva, Km 6, Route de Fès ■ 0672 73 97 78

Guests travelling with kids can opt for one of the larger hotels (see p113) instead of the smaller riads. The Coralia Club Palmariva is child-friendly with a pool, playground and an activity centre.

10 Calèche Trips
On the north side of place Foucault a ride in a horse-drawn calèche (carriage) might be a novel way to entertain kids. The carriages circle the Medina walls or go up to the Palmeraie. Prices are listed for some tours or you can negotiate an hourly rate (90 Dh is reasonable).

TOP 10 OTHER ACTIVITIES

1 Cooking
www.soukcuisine.com
Souk Cuisine organizes culinary weeks or tailor-made programmes.

2 Cycling
Bicycles can be hired across the city, including Bike Morocco at rue Khalid Ibn Eloualid in Guéliz.

3 Golf
Golf d'Amelkis: Km 12, Route de Ouarzazate; 0524 40 44 14
Play at the Palmeraie Palace (see p117) or the Golf d'Amelkis.

4 Hot-Air Ballooning
www.marrakechbyair.com
Marrakech By Air offers early morning balloon rides over the desert.

5 Tennis
MAP C5 ■ Rue Oued El Makhazine, Guéliz ■ 0524 43 19 02 ■ www.rtcma.com
The Royal Tennis Club welcomes non-members (with reservations).

6 Karting
MAP C4 ■ 0661 23 76 87
Atlas Karting on the Route de Safi also offers quad bike rides.

7 Mountain Biking
www.marrakechbikeaction.com
In addition to full-on rough-terrain biking, MBA offers city rides.

8 Marathons
www.marathon-marrakech.com
A marathon and a half marathon take place in January.

9 Skiing
When there is snow, head for Oukaimeden in the Ourika Valley (see p63).

10 Quad Biking
www.dunesdesert.com
Dunes & Desert is one of many offering exciting quad bike adventures.

Quad biking in the desert

⑩ Nightlife

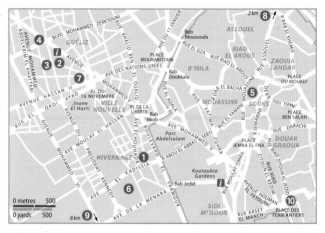

① Comptoir Darna

A spacious lounge located above the ground-floor restaurant (see p83), with a long cocktail bar, this is the place where everyone dresses up for the evening. The atmosphere is sophisticated and elegant. There are also nightly shows featuring dance troupes, Gnawa singers or orchestras performing traditional Arab music.

Diners at Comptoir Darna

② Kechmara

This hip café-bar has a friendly, relaxed vibe. In addition to live music and art installations, there is beer on tap and a large food menu (see p83).

③ Sky Bab

MAP B5 ▪ Cnr blvd Mansour Eddahbi and rue Mohammed El Beqqal, Guéliz ▪ www.babhotel marrakech.ma

This rooftop bar, found at the stylish boutique Bab Hotel in central Guéliz, is spacious and cool in every sense of the word. There are DJs at the weekend and, on occasion, live music. Visitors can also order food from the tapas menu at the restaurant downstairs.

④ Sky Bar

MAP B5 ▪ 89 Angle bld Zerktouni and Mohammed V, Guéliz

Situated on the roof of La Renaissance Hotel in the heart of Guéliz, this is one of the most buzzing bars in town at the weekend. Seven storeys above place Abdel Moumen Ben Ali, it offers terrific views down Mohammed V back to the Medina. On a clear day, you can see the Atlas mountains.

⑤ Café Arabe

Due to the presence of several saints' shrines, the serving of alcohol in the Medina is severely restricted, limited to just a handful of venues that predominantly cater to foreign

travellers. The casual Café Arabe
(see p77) serves Moroccan and
Italian food but you can drink
without eating on one of its
terraces or in the courtyard.

⑥ Théatro
**MAP C6 ■ Hotel Es Saadi,
ave El Kadissia, Hivernage ■ 0664 86
03 39 ■ Open 11pm–5am daily
■ www.theatromarrakech.com
■ MC, V accepted**

Set in a converted music hall, this
chic, popular nightclub is known for
its uproarious hedonism. The former
stage is now a busy dance floor,
with a full schedule of resident
and international DJs, and hip-hop
acts. Advance booking is
recommended.

⑦ Grand Café de la Poste
This beautifully converted
villa was originally a French-colonial-
era post office. It has a brasserie-like
feel and does a busy lunch and
dinner menu, but in the early evening,
the terrace out front is the ideal
place for a sundowner by the place
du 16 Novembre *(see p83)*.

⑧ Nikki Beach
**Circuit de la Palmeraie ■ 0663
51 99 92 ■ Open Mar–Jan:
11:30am–8pm daily ■ www.
nikkibeach.com ■ MC, V accepted**

Lounge by the pool and swim out to
the "floating bars" at this fabulously
glitzy club just 15 minutes from the
Medina. Although it closes at 8pm,
this is a popular spot for an early-
evening drink.

The pool at Nikki Beach

The main dance floor at Pacha

⑨ Pacha
**Blvd Mohammed VI, Zone
hôtelière de l'Aguedal ■ 0524 37 22
32 ■ Open noon–5am daily
■ www.pachamarrakech.com
■ MC, V accepted**

A ten-minute drive south of town,
this is North Africa's largest
superclub. It has a chillout lounge,
two restaurants and a swimming
pool with sunbathing terrace. Guest
DJs are flown in every weekend.
The enormous ballroom is also
used for major events including
the Marrakech film festival.

⑩ Kosybar
In the heart of the Medina, this
establishment has a ground floor with
a piano, a first floor with cosy nooks,
and a popular roof terrace *(see p71)*.

TOP10 Moroccan Cuisine

A colourful Moroccan salad

1 Moroccan Salads
 Moroccan salads are traditionally served at the start of a meal. Orange blossom water, a signature local ingredient, is used in the preparation of some salads.

2 Mint Tea
The ubiquitous green tea made with fresh mint leaves is invariably served with vast quantities of sugar. The technique of pouring is almost as crucial as the drink itself; the long, curved teapot spout allows the tea to be poured theatrically, and the tradition is to have three glasses each.

Mint tea

3 Set Meals
In cheaper restaurants set meals consist of a starter (soup or a salad), a main dish and a dessert (fruit or crème caramel). The more expensive restaurants serve a seemingly limitless succession of courses with more food than you could possibly eat. Indulge in such an experience at least once for a true taste of Marrakech.

4 Briouats
Small triangles of filo pastry filled with a variety of flavours – the most common are spiced minced lamb with pine nuts and feta cheese with spinach. Some kitchens in Marrakech also prepare them with shrimp, chicken and lemon. A sweet version, filled with groundnuts and soaked in honey, is widely available.

5 Couscous
A staple cuisine across North Africa, couscous comprises tiny grains of semolina that are cooked by steaming, causing them to swell and turn light and fluffy. It is usually eaten with a spicy, harissa-flavoured broth and served with steamed vegetables and meat.

6 Pastilla
Pastilla is a starter as well as a main dish. It is a pillow of filo pastry filled with a sweet and savoury stuffing – generally shredded pigeon cooked with onions and a range of spices. The dish is dusted all over with cinnamon and sugar for a distinctive Moroccan flavour.

A pigeon-stuffed *pastilla*

7 Entertainment

Some restaurants combine dining with entertainment, such as belly dancing or performances by Gnawa musicians. Chez Ali, north of Tensift Bridge, takes kitsch to extremes with fantasia horse riders, acrobats and snake charmers displaying their skills to diners.

8 Harira

A traditional Moroccan soup made with tomatoes, lentils, chickpeas, spices and lamb, this is a substantial meal by itself. Associated with special occasions, it is served during Ramadan when it is eaten at sundown to break the fast.

A comforting bowl of harira

9 Moroccan Pastries

The end of a meal is often marked with a serving of pastries. The popular honey cakes or *chabakia*, deep-fried and dipped in honey, are served during Ramadan. Another tasty dessert is sweet *pastilla* – a filo pastry covered in nuts and *crème anglaise* (custard).

10 Tajines

Cooked slowly at a low temperature in a clay pot with a cone-shaped lid that gives the dish its name, a tajine typically combines meat with fruits. Ingredients for these stewed dishes include any foodstuff that braises well, such as fish, beef, dried fruits, olives and vegetables.

TOP 10 VARIATIONS ON A TAJINE

Beef with fennel and peas

1 Beef with fennel and peas
The chefs at La Maison Arabe's Le Restaurant *(see p77)* make good use of beef in this extremely tasty tajine.

2 Lamb, onions and almonds
This savoury lamb tajine is a classic in Marrakech.

3 Lamb and dates
Served at Le Tanjia *(see p71)* and widely used in French cuisine.

4 Lamb and pear
Soft and tender, the pear is cooked so that it all but melts to the consistency of a purée.

5 Veal and green peas
The added saffron and ginger give this tajine a very special taste.

6 Lamb, prune and roast almonds
The sliced almonds add crunch to the sticky consistency of the prunes.

7 Veal and quince
Those who like a mixture of sweet and sour should try this popular tajine.

8 Fish
Apart from at Dar Moha *(see p77)*, you will find the best, freshest fish tajines in Essaouira.

9 Lamb and artichokes
Strong-flavoured seasoned lamb works beautifully with caramelised onions and fresh artichokes.

10 Kefta tajine
These are small balls of spicy minced meat that are cooked slowly in a rich tomato sauce. An egg is occasionally added to the dish.

Kefta tajine

🔟 Restaurants

Dining area at Le Foundouk

 Le Foundouk
This stylish restaurant serves fine French and Moroccan cuisine. The old courtyard building has been given a modern look, complete with leather seating and a wonderful chandelier. With a small bar area and a beautiful roof terrace, it's easy to find the perfect spot for an apéritif while waiting for a table *(see p77)*.

2 Comptoir Darna
Located in a two-storey villa, this is the best venue for a night out. The noise levels are high, with voices competing with the DJ, the food is good, with Moroccan and French choices, but it is the atmosphere that makes Comptoir Darna truly memorable – especially at weekends when there are belly dancers *(see p83)*.

 Al Fassia
This completely female-run Moroccan restaurant is unusual in that it offers à la carte choices rather than a set menu. The restaurant has a charming garden but lacks the panache of its many competitors, though it compensates with its terrific local food *(see p83)*.

4 Nomad
The clean, modern lines and restrained colour palate of this restaurant are echoed in the menu, which favours fresh, contemporary flavours as traditional Moroccan dishes are given a modern makeover. It also does superb cocktails, while profits from the daily special go to a local charity *(see p77)*.

5 Pepe Nero
Many Marrakech restaurants have beautiful riad settings but this is definitely one of the most attractive, with seating around a rose-petal-strewn pool. The mixed menu of Italian and Moroccan dishes may raise eyebrows, but the food is every bit as beguiling and assured as the spectacular setting *(see p71)*

The rooftop at Pepe Nero

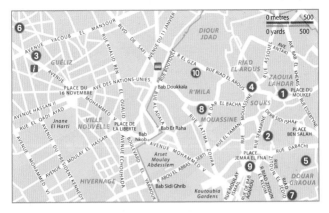

6 Amal

A charity that supports disadvantaged women, non-profit Amal provides lunches of "home-cooked" Moroccan food. The menu is limited to daily specials but the food is outstanding and offers terrific value. A little out of the way, the restaurant is five minutes' walk north of central Guéliz (see p83).

7 La Famille

In the noisy heart of the Medina, this restaurant provides peaceful respite to the hustle and bustle, with its cool courtyard filled with banana and olive trees. The seasonal vegetarian menu focuses on inventive Mediterranean cuisine, specialising in fresh, zesty salads (see p77).

8 Dar Moha

Taste Moroccan cuisine with a modern twist by Marrakech's celebrity chef Moha Fedal. The innovative food here is unlike anything else you will eat in the city. Musicians add to the ambience and perform by the candlelit pool during summer (see p77).

9 Jemaa el Fna

Each evening a part of the main square in the Medina is transformed into a vast open-air eatery. People flit between the numerous makeshift kitchens that have been set up to serve the crowds, and it is possible to sample most Moroccan classics, from harira and brochettes to couscous and tajines (see pp14–15).

A food stall at Jemaa el Fna

10 Latitude 31

Offering a modern take on Moroccan cuisine, the menu here has a lot of outwardly familiar items, including briouettes, pastilla and tajines. But the kitchen shows real invention with the ingredients and flavour combinations. The plating is exquisite and the setting is simply gorgeous – a garden courtyard just off one of the busiest alleys in the northern Medina (see p77).

TOP 10 Day Trips

1 Country Markets

Several small villages in the vicinity of Marrakech host weekly markets, with villagers from surrounding regions flocking to buy and sell produce, cheap clothing and assorted bric-a-brac. Cattle auctions are also common, as are makeshift salons of travelling barbers and dentists. Donkeys and mules are the dominant means of transport. Ask your hotel for details on where and when to find them.

2 Setti Fatma
MAP C2

This small hidden village is a 90-minute drive to the south of the city. Here, at the head of the Ourika Valley in the foothills of the Atlas Mountains, visitors will find the starting point for a 15-minute stroll up to a fine waterfall and pool. Beyond this is a strenuous hike up a steep, rocky valley to six more waterfalls.

3 Tin Mal

About a two-hour drive south of Marrakech on R203, the ancient mosque of Tin Mal makes for a stunning day out if a full trip over the Tizi-n-Test pass is not possible. Travel on a Saturday and you can stop at Asni's weekly market en route *(see p94)*.

Cascades d'Ouzoud

4 Cascades d'Ouzoud
MAP D1 ■ Riad Cascades d'Ouzoud ■ 0523 42 91 73 ■ www.ouzoud.com

Two hours northeast on the Route de Fès, these are the most beautiful waterfalls in Morocco. Take a trek through wooded groves *(ouzoud is Berber for olives)* to reach the gorges of Oued El Abid. There is a lovely riad at the top of the cascades if you fancy spending the night.

5 Essaouira

This medieval walled port-city on the Atlantic coast is only a few hours' drive from Marrakech. It has beaches, ramparts, souks, a fishing harbour and a fascinating hippy-era history *(see pp86–91)*.

6 Tameslohte
MAP C1

A 30-minute drive out of Marrakech on the Route d'Amizmiz, Tameslohte is a roadside village famed

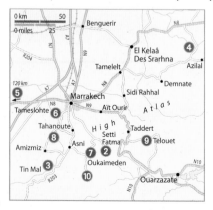

for its busy potters' cooperative. There are also weavers' workshops, an ancient mule-driven olive oil press and a crumbling kasbah. Start the trip with a visit to the Association Tameslohte – a useful information office on the main square, place Sour Souika, next to the main mosque. If the office is shut, one of the locals will be able to tell you where to find the potters.

7 Oukaimeden
MAP C2

For part of the year, Marrakech serves as a base for skiers. Snowfall on the Atlas between February and April means business for the ski resort at Oukaimeden, high above the Ourika Valley. There is a chairlift and ski equipment can be hired on site. In spring and summer, visitors can see the Bronze Age petroglyphs.

8 Barrage Lalla Takerkoust
MAP C2 ■ Le Flouka, BP 45 Barrage Lalla Takerkoust ■ 0664 49 26 60 ■ www.leflouka-marrakech.com

Found to the south of Marrakech on the Route d'Amizmiz, this impressive artificial lake is backed by the beautiful Atlas Mountains. The clear water makes it a great place to go swimming and visitors can take out one of the boats for hire. Try the local cuisine at one of the many waterside restaurants, including Le Flouka, which also offers accommodation.

Skiing at Oukaimeden

9 Kasbah Telouet

Travellers to Ouarzazate invariably call at the imposing mountain palace of Telouet, but if your plans don't include a trip south of the Atlas, then visit the kasbah on a day trip from Marrakech. A daily bus goes to Telouet or you can hire a taxi for the day – ask your hotel to arrange it (see p99).

10 Kasbah du Toubkal

A former tribal stronghold deep in the Atlas Mountains, this traditional kasbah is set at the foot of Jbel Toubkal (see p93). The last part of the journey is done by mule. Visitors are brought up for a Berber lunch and hike, and are delivered back into town before dark. It is possible to stay overnight at the kasbah (see p97).

Kasbah du Toubkal

Marrakech
Area by Area

The UNESCO World Heritage Site
Kasbah Aït Benhaddou

TOP 10 Jemaa el Fna and the Kasbah

Dar Si Said Museum detail

The spiritual and historical heart of Marrakech, the Jemaa el Fna (pronounced as a rushed "j'maf na"), was laid out as a parade ground by the founders of the city *(see pp12–15)*. Marrakech's next rulers constructed a walled royal domain to the south – known as the Kasbah – and the open ground passed into the public domain. Sultans and royal palaces have come and gone, but the Jemaa el Fna remains eternally vital. Once used to display the heads of executed criminals, it is still home to some extra-ordinary sights, such as snake charmers and tooth pullers. By night, it transforms into a food market.

JEMAA EL FNA AND THE KASBAH

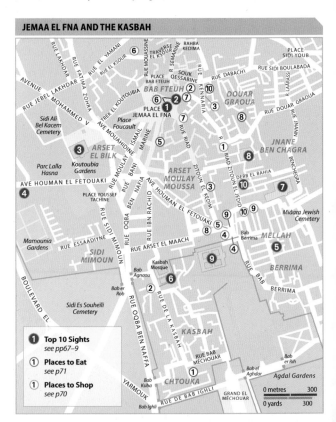

1 Top 10 Sights
see pp67–9

① Places to Eat
see p71

① Places to Shop
see p70

0 metres   300
0 yards   300

1 Jemaa el Fna
MAP J3

One of the most spectacular squares in North Africa, Jemaa el Fna throngs with entertainers, as well as enthralled visitors and locals. Running south off Jemma el Fna, Rue de Bab Agnaou is the Medina's pedestrianized "modern" main street, where you can find ATMs, internet cafés and pharmacies. Its narrow side alleys are home to good-value hotels (see pp12–13).

2 Night Market
MAP J3

Early evening brings a change to Jemaa el Fna as the nightly food market takes over the square and fills the air with the aroma of grilling meat. Nearby is the Rue Riad Zitoun el Jedid, which connects several major sights with Jemaa el Fna, including the Dar Si Said Museum. Rue Riad Zitoun el Kedim links Jemaa el Fna with the palace quarter (see pp14–15).

3 Koutoubia Mosque

The Koutoubia Mosque is easily identified by its magnificent minaret (tower). This beautiful structure reaches a towering height of 77 m (252 ft), its rose-pink colour makes for an eye-catching contrast, silhouetted against the cobalt blue of the sky by day and the fiery orange of twilight in the early evening (see pp20–21). However, only Muslims are permitted inside the mosque.

Koutoubia Mosque

4 La Mamounia Hotel
MAP H5

This former palace has been one of Marrakech's landmark hotels since it opened in 1923. You don't have to be a guest to enjoy its smart poolside bar and restaurant – as long as you dress the part (see pp34–5).

Al Mamoun Suite, La Mamounia Hotel

5 The Mellah
MAP L5

The old Jewish quarter lies immediately east of the Kasbah. Visitors can enter via the Souk El Bab Salaam, a busy, covered market street across from a rose-planted square. The street leads to place Souweka and to the north you'll find one of the city's last working synagogues. Most of Marrakech's Jewish population left for Israel after World War II, in the 1950s and 1960s, but the number of graves in the nearby Miâara Jewish cemetery is testament to how many once lived here.

6 Saadian Tombs

The historic Saadian tombs are located down a narrow alley that runs beside the Kasbah Mosque, which itself is just inside the beautiful and equally historic Bab Agnaou *(see p25)*. The small garden site is the resting place for some 66 royals of the Saadian dynasty, whose reign marked a golden era in the history of the city *(see pp26–7)*.

Saadian Tombs and garden

7 Bahia Palace

MAP K5 ■ 5 rue Riad Zitoun El Jedid ■ 0524 38 91 79 ■ Open 8:30–11:45am, 2:30–5:45pm Sat–Thu, 8:30–11:30am, 3–5:45pm Fri ■ Adm

Built in the 1890s by a powerful grand vizier (high official), the Bahia ("Brilliant") is an impressive minor palace complex approached by a long garden driveway. Inside, arrows direct visitors through a succession of courtyards and private rooms that were used by the vizier and his four wives. All of the rooms are lavishly decorated with *zellij* tiling *(see p45)*, sculpted stucco and carved cedarwood. The ruling sultan, Abdel Aziz, was so jealous of the riches of the Bahia that on the vizier's death he had parts of the palace stripped.

8 Dar Si Said Museum

MAP K4 ■ Rue Riad Zitoun El Jedid ■ 0524 38 95 64 ■ Open 9am–5pm Wed–Mon ■ Adm

Built by the brother of Ba Ahmed, builder of the Bahia Palace, this is an altogether more modest dwelling. However, what it sacrifices in scale, it more than makes up for in its impressive detailing – the house has some beautiful painted ceilings. It also serves as a museum for decorative arts; the exhibits on display include fine examples of carved wooden panels and painted Berber doors. The museum also houses some interestingly designed jewellery, carpets and metalwork.

9 Badii Palace

It is difficult to reconcile these ruins with a palace once reputed to be among the world's finest. An expanse of dusty ground within half-eroded walls, it retains some of its original elements, including sunken gardens and dazzling Moorish craftsmanship *(see pp30–31)*.

Bahia Palace decoration

Exhibits at Musée Tiskiwin

⑩ Musée Tiskiwin
MAP K4 ▪ 8 derb El Bahia, off rue Riad Zitoun El Jedid ▪ 0524 38 91 92 ▪ Open 9am–12:30pm, 2:30–6pm daily ▪ Adm

Located en route to the Dar Si Said Museum, this is a private house belonging to the Dutch anthropologist Bert Flint. An avid documenter of tribal arts and crafts, Flint amassed a fascinating and vast collection. Presented in his home for public viewing, the exhibition has been organized geographically as a journey that traces the old desert trade routes all the way from Marrakech to Timbuktu. Exhibit labels are in French, but there is an English guidebook.

THE KING AND HIS PALACES
Throughout Moroccan history, the royal court has shifted base between Marrakech, Fès, Meknès and Rabat. The Almohads constructed Marrakech's first royal palace in the 12th century to the south of Jemaa el Fna and it has been there ever since. The present King Mohammed VI had a smaller palace built for his personal use, outside the Bab Agnaou.

TO THE PALACES

▶ MORNING
Start on Jemaa el Fna (see pp12–15). On the southern side is an arch that leads to rue Riad Zitoun El Kedim (see p67). This area is mainly inhabited by locals and there is a distinct absence of souvenir and trinket vendors. At the southern end of the street, several places sell items that are fashioned out of old car tyres – from the purely practical (buckets) to the quirky (stylish mirror frames). Across the main road is the Marché Couvert (see p70), a fruit, vegetable and meat market that's worth a quick look. Just southeast is the place des Ferblantiers (see p70), a paved plaza surrounded by metal-workers with a gate that leads through to the haunting Badii Palace. After visiting the ruins, grab a cheap snack from one of the stalls on the northwest corner of place des Ferblantiers.

AFTERNOON
Wander through the Souk El Bab Salaam (see p70) before heading back north up the rue Riad Zitoun El Jedid (see p67). At the end of the street, on the right, is the gateway to the Bahia Palace, but anyone pushed for time should instead turn right and take the first left to the excellent Dar Si Said Museum. Just south is the equally interesting Musée Tiskiwin. Return to rue Riad Zitoun El Jedid and continue north where you will eventually pass the Cinéma Eden, one of the city's few open-air picture houses, and bear left to re-emerge onto the lively Jemaa el Fna.

See map on p66 ←

Places to Shop

A woman walks past Moroccan carpets on rue Riad Zitoun El Jedid

1 Rue Riad Zitoun El Jedid
MAP K4

This street is lined with small, interesting boutiques. It is a pleasant alternative to the souks.

2 ETS Bouchaib

This vast government-run storehouse is close to the Saadian Tombs. You'll find traditional Moroccan handicrafts at fixed prices here, so no haggling (see p27).

3 Warda la Mouche
MAP K3 ∎ 127 rue Kennaria
∎ 0524 38 90 63

A small boutique selling hand-made contemporary Franco-Moroccan-style women's clothing. It also sells scarves and accessories.

4 Place des Ferblantiers
MAP K5

As an alternative to the souks, this is the place to go to for unique brass and iron lanterns that come in all shapes and sizes.

Brass lantern

5 Aya's
MAP K5 ∎ 11 bis, derb Jdid, Bab Mellah ∎ www.ayasmarrakech.com

It may be hard to find (a door away from Le Tanjia), but it is worth seeking out for exotic clothing, jewellery and accessories.

6 AlNour
MAP J3 ∎ Derb Moulay El Ghali 19 ∎ 0524 39 03 23

This social enterprise boutique features exquisite accessories and hand-embroidered clothing made with natural fibers, crafted by local women.

7 Le Cadeau Berbère
MAP J3 ∎ 51 Jemaa el Fna
∎ 0524 44 29 07

Established in 1930, this family-run textile specialist has an international clientele that includes interior designers, hoteliers and collectors.

8 Marché Couvert
MAP K5 ∎ Ave Houman El Fetouaki ∎ Closed Fri

Commonly called the Mellah Market, this indoor market sells flowers, household goods and local produce.

9 Atelier El Bahia
MAP K5 ∎ Rue Bahia Bab Mellah ∎ 0524 38 52 86

Even if you're not in the market for a new rug, you can still browse the shelves full of handmade shawls, throws and soft furnishings.

10 Souk El Bab Salaam
MAP K5

Follow the aromas wafting from the edge of the old Jewish quarter to this small herb and spice market.

Places to Eat

PRICE CATEGORIES
For a full meal for one with half a bottle of wine (or equivalent meal), plus taxes and extra charges.

Dh under 200 Dh   Dh Dh 200–400 Dh
Dh Dh Dh over 400 Dh

1 Café Clock
MAP K7 ■ 224 derb Chtouka, Kasbah ■ 0524 37 83 67 ■ Open 9am–10pm daily ■ Dh

Serving camel burgers, almond milkshakes, home-made ice cream and all-day Berber breakfasts.

2 Le Marrakchi
MAP K3 ■ 52 rue des Banques ■ 0524 44 33 77 ■ Open noon–midnight daily ■ www.lemarrakchi. com ■ MC, V accepted ■ Dh Dh Dh

This restaurant has a lively roof terrace, with music and belly dancing.

3 Zwin Zwin Café
MAP K4 ■ 4 rue Riad Zitoun El Kedim ■ 0524 38 07 07 ■ Open 11:30am–11pm daily ■ MC, V accepted ■ Dh

This chic café with a roof terrace is run by a French woman. Alcohol served.

4 Kosybar
MAP K5 ■ 47 place des Ferblantiers ■ 0524 38 03 24 ■ Open 11am–1am daily ■ MC, V accepted ■ Dh Dh Dh

Eat Japanese-Mediterranean fusion on the lovely, cool terrace or in the exotic interior.

5 Pâtisserie des Princes
MAP J4 ■ 32 rue de Bab Agnaou ■ 0524 44 30 33 ■ Open 6am–11pm daily

A local version of a French pastry parlour, this place also offers ice creams, juices, tea and coffee.

6 Jemaa el Fna
For the ultimate dining experience, try one of the stalls in the square (see pp14–15).

7 Chez Chegrouni
MAP K3 ■ Jemaa el Fna ■ 0665 47 46 15 ■ Open 6am–11pm daily ■ No credit cards ■ Dh

Dine on tasty, well-priced local dishes. Sit on the roof terrace and enjoy the view.

8 Pepe Nero
MAP K4 ■ 12 derb Cherkaoui, Douar Graoua ■ 0524 38 90 67 ■ Open noon–2:30pm, 7:30–11pm Tue–Sun ■ www.pepenero-marrakech. com ■ Dh Dh Dh Dh

Excellent high-end Italian-Moroccan, worth splashing out on (see p60).

High-end dining at Pepe Nero

9 Le Tanjia
MAP K5 ■ 14 derb Jedid, Hay Essalam, Mellah ■ 0524 38 38 36 ■ Open 11am–midnight daily ■ Credit cards accepted ■ Dh Dh Dh

A three-floored temple of fine dining and entertainment with an excellent Moroccan menu and belly dancers.

10 Roti d'Or
MAP K3 ■ 17 rue Kennaria, Medina ■ 0627 13 11 37 ■ Open noon–4pm, 6–8:30pm Sat–Thu ■ Dh

A small but hip pavement café offering burgers, tacos and wraps prepared with a Moroccan twist.

See map on p66 ←

TOP 10 **The Souks**

North of Jemaa el Fna is a vast area of tightly squeezed commerce with dozens of narrow alleyways. These passageways are lined with shops the size of cupboards selling cloth, leather, metalwork, brass lanterns, carpets and jewellery. Each area is dedicated to a single item, so a street may be packed with sellers of nothing but canary-yellow leather slippers, while another is filled with vendors of glazed pottery. Don't fall for the sellers' flattering cry, "Hey my friend, for you I give special price": it always pays to haggle. Irrespective of whether you are buying or not, it is an entrancing experience.

Mouassine Fountain

1 **Mouassine Fountain**
MAP J2

There are two main routes into the souks: rue Mouassine and rue Semmarine. The former runs past the Mouassine Mosque, after which the neighbourhood is named. A right turn at the mosque leads to a small plaza that holds a fountain with four bays – three for animals and one for humans. An arched gateway next to the fountain leads to the Souk des Teinturiers (see p73).

2 **Dar Cherifa**
MAP J2 ▪ 8 derb Charfa Lakbir, Mouassine ▪ 0524 42 65 50 ▪ Open 10am–11pm daily ▪ www.dar-cherifa.com

This beautifully renovated town house can be located by following the signs on the alley opposite the Mouassine Mosque. Featuring exquisite wood-work and carved plasterwork, some of the interiors date back to the 16th century. The house operates as a cultural centre, restaurant and *salon de thé* (tearoom).

3 **Fondouks**
MAP J2 ▪ 192 rue Mouassine

To the north of the Mouassine Mosque, past Café Arabe (see p77), is an excellent example of a *fondouk* – an old merchants' hostel. The rooms on the ground floor are used as workshops and the ones upstairs are mainly used for storage.

THE SOUKS

This particular *fondouk* had a brush with stardom when it featured in the 1998 film *Hideous Kinky*, as the hotel where actress Kate Winslet and her daughters are shown to be staying.

④ Souk des Teinturiers

One of the most alluring places in Marrakech, the Dyers' Souk is a tangle of narrow alleyways east of the Mouassine Mosque. It becomes a riot of colours during the day, when hanks of just-dyed wools are hung out to dry above certain alleys. The dyers themselves are very easy to identify; they are the men with bright red, purple and blue colours up to their elbows *(see p16)*.

Dyed wool hanging in Souk des Teinturiers

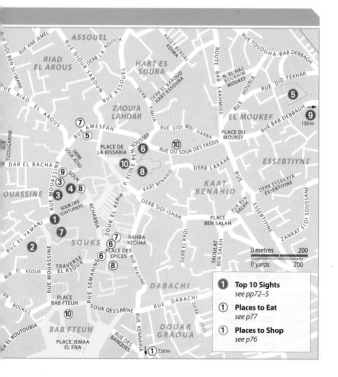

①	**Top 10 Sights** see pp72–5
①	**Places to Eat** see p77
①	**Places to Shop** see p76

The wonderfully colourful, but overwhelmingly pungent, tanneries

5 The Tanneries
MAP L1

A strong stomach is required to visit this particular quarter of the Medina. This is where animal hides are turned into leather. The work is done by hand as the hides are soaked in open vats. They look like a paintbox of watercolours from a distance, but up close smell so foul that guides give visitors sprigs of mint to hold under their noses. The tanneries are scheduled to move location as a result of the pollution they cause. If you venture this far, pay a visit to the nearby Bab Debbagh (see p25).

6 Medersa Ben Youssef

Located north of the Musée de Marrakech, this is a beautiful building. A 16th-century theological college, it has tiny, windowless cells designed to house several hundred students. The central courtyard, which combines polychromic tiling, decorative plasterwork and wood panelling to sublime effect, is its most stunning feature (see pp28–9).

7 Musée Douiria de Mouassine
MAP J2 ■ 4–5 derb el Hammam, Mouassine ■ 0524 37 77 92 ■ Open 9:30am–7pm daily ■ Adm ■ www. museedemouassine.com

A remarkable discovery was unearthed at this otherwise modest first-floor apartment. Hidden beneath the plaster were extraordinary painted ceilings and panels. It emerged that this had been the residence of a Saadian noble and below the later accretions, its 16th-century architecture and decor remained intact. Visitors can view the ongoing restoration work, visit temporary exhibitions and take tea at the rooftop café.

8 Musée de Marrakech
MAP K2 ■ Place Ben Youssef ■ 0524 44 18 93 ■ Open 9am–6:30pm daily (except religious holidays) ■ Adm ■ www.musee.ma

This splendid 19th-century palace houses the Fondation Omar Benjelloun, which features ethnological and archaeological material as well as a wide-ranging collection of ancient and contemporary artwork. The

Courtyard, Musée de Marrakech

former *hammam* makes an unusual exhibition space. Books, tea, coffee and pastries are also sold here.

9 City Walls and Gates
MAP K2

The city walls and gates, built around the 1120s, surround the Medina. While Bab Agnaou, which is located to the west of the Saadian Tombs is considered to be the most beautiful, Bab Debbagh gives you access to the tanneries. The internal staircase at Bab Debbagh leads to a roof from which you can enjoy stunning, panoramic views of the city.

The ancient Koubba El Badiyin

10 Koubba El Badiyin
MAP K2 ■ Place Ben Youssef
■ 0524 44 18 93

This fully intact building from the 11th century is the only remaining example of Almoravid architecture in the city. Built by the Almoravid dynasty, it is assumed to be the ablutions area for the Medersa Ben Youssef. It is currently being renovated, but the intricate motifs and battlements can easily be admired from the street.

THE SEVEN SAINTS

Marrakech has seven patron saints – all of whom are believed to be sleeping to one day rise again. The Medina is dotted with the green-roofed shrines of the saints. These are all off limits to non-Muslims, though it is possible to walk through the outer precincts of the Shrine of Sidi Bel Abbes. Once a year, pilgrims flood to visit a shrine a day.

HIDDEN MARRAKECH

▶ MORNING

Wrong turns and too many distractions make it impossible to plan a walk through the souks, which you should explore independently. On another day, head up rue Mouassine and take a left opposite the Mouassine Mosque before taking the first right to **Dar Cherifa** *(see p72)*. Return to rue Mouassine and turn left at the T-junction. Take the first right through a low archway; follow the alley left and then right to No. 22 and ring the bell for the eccentric **Ministero del Gusto**, a studio and gallery *(by appointment only)*. Back on the main street, take a left towards the **Mouassine Fountain** *(see p72)* or detour for a look at the **Musée Douiria de Mousassine**. Head north up rue Mouassine and stop at the **Café Arabe** *(see p77)* for lunch.

AFTERNOON

After the café is the **fondouk** made famous in *Hideous Kinky* starring Kate Winslet *(see p72)*. Bear left onto rue Dar El Bacha, named for the Dar El Bacha palace, the former residence of Thami El Glaoui *(see p39 and p100)*, the much-feared ruler of Marrakech and southern Morocco during the first half of the 20th century. It is currently closed to the public but the street has many excellent antique emporia. Continue past the Bab Doukkala Mosque, through a street market to the **Bab Doukkala gate** *(see p25)* and exit the Medina; you could walk on to Guéliz or catch a taxi back to Jemaa el Fna.

See map on pp72–3

Places to Shop

1 Mustapha Blaoui
MAP H2 ■ 142 rue Bab Doukkala ■ 0524 38 52 40
Monsieur Blaoui's warehouse of Moroccan goods has everything from candleholders to wardrobes.

Moroccan goods, Mustapha Blaoui

2 Ensemble Artisanal
MAP H3 ■ Ave Mohammed V ■ 0524 44 35 03
A government store of Moroccan handicrafts. Though not as much fun as the souks, it is less stressful.

3 Kulchi
MAP J3 ■ 15 derb Nkhel ■ 0639 22 12 59 ■ www.kulchi.com
A fashion-mag-friendly, Australian-owned business selling gorgeous carpets, hand-woven blankets, ceramics and other objects. By appointment.

4 Kif Kif
MAP J3 ■ 8 rue des Ksours ■ 0661 08 20 41
This shop sells ethno-chic gifts including a range of wares made by women's cooperatives. Kif Kif also distributes old clothes and supports local charities.

Sack slippers, Souk Cherifia

5 Max & Jan
MAP K2 ■ 14 rue Amsefah, Sidi Abdelaziz ■ 0524 37 55 70 ■ www.maxandjan.ma
From their flagship boutique in the Medina, Swiss-Belgian duo Max and Jan bring an international edge to Moroccan design.

6 Chabi Chic
MAP K3 ■ 1 derb Arjaan, off Rahba Kedima ■ 0524 38 15 46
Located within Nomad restaurant, this attractive boutique sells traditional and contemporary handmade pottery as well as beauty products.

7 Bazar du Sud
MAP K2 ■ 14 Souk des Tapis ■ 0524 44 30 04 ■ www.bazardusud.com
Of the countless carpet shops in the souk, this has possibly the largest selection, backed up by an extremely professional sales service.

8 L'Art du Bain
MAP K3 ■ 13 Souk el Badine ■ 068 44 59 42
This store deals in handmade soaps, from the traditional Moroccan *savon noir* to natural soaps infused with rose or musk.

9 Souk Cherifia
MAP J2 ■ 184 rue Mouassine, Medina
One of the best shopping stops for designer clothes, accessories and homeware, composed of more than 20 independent boutiques.

10 Beldi
MAP J3 ■ 9–11 rue Laksour ■ 0524 44 10 76
This tiny boutique at the entrance to the souks showcases the work of brothers Toufik and Abdelhafid. They adapt Moroccan clothing for contemporary Western tastes to stunning effect.

Places to Eat

PRICE CATEGORIES
For a full meal for one with half a bottle of wine (or equivalent meal), plus taxes and extra charges.

Dh under 200 Dh   Dh Dh 200–400 Dh
Dh Dh Dh over 400 Dh

1 La Famille
MAP K4 ■ 42 rue Riad Zitoun el Jdid ■ 0524 38 52 95 ■ Open noon–5pm Tue–Sun ■ Cards accepted ■ Dh

Enjoy fresh vegetarian Mediterranean cuisine in the cool shade of this tranquil garden restaurant that comes as a surprise in the bustle of the Medina.

2 La Maison Arabe
Elegant Moroccan cuisine in the main restaurant (see p112). French, Moroccan and Asian in Les Trois Saveurs.

3 Café Arabe
MAP J2 ■ 184 rue Mouassine ■ 0524 42 97 28 ■ Open 10am–11pm daily ■ Dh Dh

Italian and Moroccan food is served on the pillow-strewn roof terrace.

4 Henna Café
MAP H2 ■ 93 Arset Aouzal, off rue Bab Doukkala ■ 0656 56 63 74 ■ Open 11am–8pm daily ■ Dh

Traditional snacks and beverages, with local women who will paint your hands with beautiful henna designs.

5 Dar Moha
MAP H2 ■ 81 rue Dar El Bacha ■ 0524 38 64 00/38 62 64 ■ Open noon–4pm, 7:30–10pm daily ■ AmEx, MC, V accepted ■ Dh Dh Dh

Sit by the pool and enjoy the exceptional food (see p61).

6 Café des Epices
MAP K3 ■ 75 Rahba Lakdima ■ 0524 39 17 70 ■ Open 9am–11pm daily ■ No credit cards ■ Dh

Calm and charming, this café offers a welcome break from the souk.

7 Atay Café
MAP K2 ■ 62 rue Amesfah, Sidi Abdelaziz■ 0661 34 42 46 ■ Open 10am–10pm daily ■ Dh

A beautiful, friendly little café with three terraces. As well as Moroccan staples, it serves dishes like ravioli, salads and juices.

8 Nomad
MAP K3 ■ 1 derb Arjaan, off Rahba Kedima ■ 0524 38 16 09 ■ Open 11am–11pm daily ■ Cards accepted ■ Dh Dh

Excellent contemporary restaurant (see p60) owned by the same people behind Café des Épices and Terrasse des Épices above the Souk Cherifia.

9 Latitude 31
MAP H1 ■ 186 rue El Gza, Arset Ihiri, Bab Doukkala ■ 0524 38 49 34 ■ Open 6–11pm Mon–Sat ■ Cards accepted ■ Dh Dh

Innovative Moroccan cuisine in a beautiful setting (see p61). A good option for lovers of fish (the seafood tajine is a must). No alcohol.

Le Foundouk roof terrace at dusk

10 Le Foundouk
MAP K2 ■ 55 rue du Souk des Fassis ■ 0524 37 81 90 ■ Open 7pm–midnight Thu–Tue ■ MC, V accepted ■ Dh Dh

Wonderfully stylish restaurant with a French-Moroccan menu. There's also a romantic roof terrace (see p60).

See map on pp72–3

TOP 10 The New City

Jnane El Harti

It was only with the arrival of the French in the early 20th century that Marrakech broke out of the walls of the Medina. The new colonial rulers built their own *ville nouvelle* of broad avenues, villas and parks. Over time, Moroccans aspiring for a better lifestyle moved out into this new town, lured by serviceable plumbing, electricity and cars. Now known as Guéliz – from *église*, French for church (the area has the city's first) – the New City has plenty for tourists looking to explore Marrakech's modern facet. The streets are lined with fine restaurants and shops, while come evening, there is a lively nightlife.

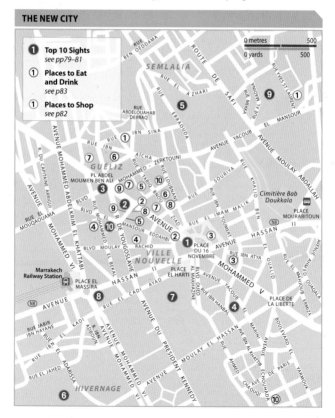

THE NEW CITY

① **Top 10 Sights**
see pp79–81

① **Places to Eat and Drink**
see p83

① **Places to Shop**
see p82

Avenue Mohammed V, a grand, palm-shaded thoroughfare through the city

1 Avenue Mohammed V
MAP C5

This wide avenue, named after Morocco's first king, is the spine of Marrakech. It connects the old and new cities, running from the Koutoubia to Jbel Guéliz (Mount Guéliz), a rocky outcrop northwest of the town. Along the way are three major roundabouts: place de la Liberté with its modern fountain; place du 16 Novembre where the main post office is located; and the heart of the New City, place Abdel Moumen Ben Ali.

2 Mauresque Architecture

The French brought with them European architectural styles, which mixed with local Moorish influences to create a new style, soon dubbed "Mauresque". Avenue Mohammed V is dotted with Mauresque structures, especially where it intersects with rue de la Liberté; here several buildings have clean Modernist lines but also have pavement arcades to shade pedestrians from the sun.

3 Hotel La Renaissance
MAP C5 ▪ 89 Angle blvd Zerktouni and Mohammed V, Guéliz ▪ 0524 33 77 77 ▪ www.renaissance-hotel-marrakech.com

Built in 1952, La Renaissance was the first hotel in the modern district

of Guéliz, and has since become an iconic building in Marrakech. The rooftop terrace offers a breathtaking panorama of the whole of the Guéliz area, and is the perfect spot to sample cocktails and take in the splendour of the Koutoubia (see p56).

4 Église des Saints-Martyrs de Marrakech
MAP C5 ▪ Rue El Imam Ali, Guéliz ▪ 0524 43 05 85 ▪ Services: 6:30pm Mon–Sat, 10am Sun

Built in 1926, this Catholic church stands as a tribute to six 13th-century Franciscan friars beheaded by the sultan as a punishment for preaching Christianity. Its spartan interior is enlivened by colourful panels of stained glass. The church's bell tower is now overshadowed by the minaret of an adjacent mosque. Protestant services are held in the library on Sunday at 10:30am.

Église des Saints-Martyrs de Marrakech

The European cemetery

5 European Cemetery
MAP C4 ■ Rue Erraouda
■ Open Apr–Sep: 7am–7pm;
Oct–Mar: 8am–6pm

North of boulevard Mohammed Zerktouni is a walled graveyard dating back to the 1920s. It is the burial ground of many of the original inhabitants of Guéliz. A dozen English Protestant missionaries also rest here. Most notable is the tomb of Kate Hosali, who founded SPANA, a charity for working animals of the world, in 1923 after being appalled by the maltreatment of Morocco's beasts of burden.

6 Hivernage
MAP C6

South of Guéliz and immediately west of the Medina walls, Hivernage is a small neighbourhood of quiet streets that are shaded by trees. Its mix of villas and a handful of five-star hotels ensures a tranquil atmosphere with light pedestrian traffic.

There are one or two fairly good restaurants in the area, in addition to the city's favourite nightspot, Comptoir Darna (see p56).

7 Jnane El Harti
MAP C5

A small and pretty park just off place du 16 Novembre, Jnane El Harti was originally laid out by the French as a formal garden and zoo. In a 1939 essay titled "Marrakech", George Orwell (see p42) writes of feeding gazelles here. Numerous notices provide information about the various species of plants growing in the many flowerbeds. The plaza fronting the park gates is popular and often used for events.

HIPPYVILLE

Before the Medina's hotel boom, those who couldn't afford La Mamounia, or considered it too representative of the establishment, stayed in Guéliz. The Es Saadi in Hivernage was popular with the Rolling Stones, while Beat writer William Burroughs shacked up at Hotel Toulousain. The big hippy hangout at the time was Hotel La Renaissance.

---

8 Théâtre Royal
MAP B5 ■ Ave Hassan II ■ 0524 43 15 16 ■ Opening times vary

This striking piece of architecture by leading local light, Charles Boccara, is crowned by a grand dome. The interior has a beautiful, tiled

Théâtre Royal

courtyard linking a 1,200-seat open-air theatre and an 800-seat opera house. The work of local artists and sculptors is occasionally displayed here.

Majorelle Gardens fountain

⑨ Majorelle Gardens

A 10-minute walk east of place Abdel Moumen Ben Ali, these gardens are the absolute must-see sight in the New City. Created in the 1920s and 1930s by the French painter Jacques Majorelle, they were owned by French couturier and part-time Morocco resident Yves Saint-Laurent until his death in 2008. Open to the public, the gardens include a museum of Berber culture, a gift shop, gallery, café and a garden memorial to YSL. Next door is the Musée Yves Saint Laurent (see pp32–3).

⑩ Spanish Quarter
MAP B5

Running west off rue de Yougoslavie is a narrow street lined with single-storey houses of a unique design, much like terraced cottages. This shady lane, planted with mulberry trees, constitutes the city's old Spanish quarter, a testament to Marrakech's once considerable Hispanic population. The small houses, formerly brightly coloured, are now a uniform Marrakech pink.

OLD CITY TO NEW CITY

▶ MORNING

Start next to the **Koutoubia Mosque** (see pp20–21) and head up **avenue Mohammed V** (see p79). After a few minutes you will come to **Arsat Moulay Abdeslem** (see p51) on the left, known as "Cyber Park" after its popular internet centre. Exit the Medina through the Bab Nkob, plunging into the large traffic island, **place de la Liberté**. Take the second left after the traffic junction, followed by the first right, and you'll find yourself in the historic **Église des Saints-Martyrs de Marrakech** (see p79). Continue north up avenue Yacoub Marini to reach **Jnane El Harti** park. Cross the place du 16 Novembre to lunch at the **Grand Café de la Poste** (see p83).

AFTERNOON

The road next to McDonald's leads to the **Marché Central** (see p82) which is well worth the 15-minute detour. Return to Mohammed V for some of the best shopping in town, particularly around **rue de la Liberté**, just past the Carré Eden shopping centre. The next major traffic intersection, place Abdel Moumen Ben Ali, is overlooked by the Parisian-style **Café Les Négociants** (see p83) which is a good place to rest your feet and enjoy a coffee or an orange juice. You are now at the heart of Guéliz; in addition to shopping, there are several interesting galleries nearby (see pp40–41), as well as excellent eating and drinking options (see p83).

See map on p78 ←

Places to Shop

1 33 Rue Majorelle
MAP C4 ■ 33 rue Yves Saint-Laurent, Guéliz ■ 0524 31 41 95
■ www.33ruemajorelle.com
Regularly changing stock from a host of Moroccan designers including clothes, accessories, jewellery and handicrafts.

Accessories at 33 Rue Majorelle

2 Place Vendôme
MAP B5 ■ 141 ave Mohammed V ■ 0524 43 52 63 ■ Open 9am–1pm, 3–7pm Mon–Sat ■ MC, V accepted
The leather items here are of much greater quality than those sold in the souks and are designed with more of an international style and flavour.

3 Marché Central
MAP C4 ■ Rue Ibn Toumert
A variety of foodstuffs are available at this market, as well as handicrafts (see p53).

4 Al Badii
MAP B5 ■ 54 blvd Moulay Rachid ■ 0524 43 16 93 ■ Closed 1–15 Aug ■ Credit cards accepted
The best shop for unusual yet stylish Moroccan furnishings, ceramics and old embroidery. It also has a

basement full of carpets and photos of celebrity shoppers on the walls.

5 Moor
MAP B5 ■ 7 rue des Vieux Marrakchis, Guéliz ■ 0524 45 82 74
■ www.akbardelightscollections.com
■ Closed Sun ■ Credit cards accepted
Sublime clothing and houseware, though it can be a little pricey.

6 Café du Livre
MAP B5 ■ 44 rue Tarik Bnou Ziad, next to Hotel Toulousain
■ 0524 44 69 21 ■ Closed Sun
■ Credit cards accepted
This haven for book lovers offers a range of interesting titles from across the globe in many languages. It also has a café with Wi-Fi access.

7 Galerie Birkemeyer
MAP B5 ■ 169–171 rue Mohammed El Bekal ■ 0524 44 69 63 ■ www.galerie-birkemeyer.com
■ Closed 15 Jul–15 Aug ■ AmEx, MC, V accepted
Great for leather goods as well as international designer sportswear.

8 L'Orientaliste
MAP B5 ■ 11 & 15 rue de la Liberté ■ 0524 43 40 74 ■ Closed Jul–Aug ■ MC, V accepted
A small shop with small items such as tea glasses and jewellery. Its basement is packed with larger pieces and antique furniture.

9 Atika Chaussures
MAP B5 ■ 34 rue de la Liberté, Guéliz ■ 0524 43 64 09 ■ Closed Sun
■ Credit cards accepted
Moccasins and loafers in myriad colours adorn this fashionable store.

10 Scènes du Lin
MAP B5 ■ 70 rue de la Liberté
■ 0524 43 61 08 ■ www.scenesdelin.com ■ Closed Aug ■ MC, V accepted
Browse through finely designed curtains with Fès embroidery and a selection of unusual lamps.

Places to Eat

1 Amal
MAP B4 ▪ Rue Allal Ben Ahmed, Guéliz ▪ 0524 44 68 96 ▪ Open noon–4pm daily ▪ No credit cards ▪ Dh

Eat heartily and support a deserving cause *(see p61)*. If you enjoy the food, sign up for a cooking class.

2 Grand Café de la Poste
MAP B5 ▪ Cnr blvd El Mansour Eddahbi & ave Imam Malik ▪ 0524 43 30 38 ▪ Open 8am–1am daily ▪ Credit cards accepted ▪ Dh Dh

The Art Deco interior of this café, built in 1925, is largely intact. The service can be patchy.

3 Eveil Des Sens
MAP C5 ▪ 32 rue Ibn Atya, Guéliz ▪ 0524 45 86 17 ▪ Dh

Unpretentious neighbourhood restaurant that supplements solid Moroccan fare with pasta and pizza. Good value and child friendly.

4 La Trattoria Marrakech
MAP B5 ▪ 179 rue Mohammed El Bekal ▪ 0524 43 26 41 ▪ Open 12–3pm, 7pm–midnight daily ▪ MC, V accepted ▪ Dh Dh

The city's best Italian restaurant is housed in a beautiful villa with seats beside the pool.

5 Kechmara
MAP B5 ▪ 3 rue de la Liberté ▪ 0524 42 25 32 ▪ Open 11:30–1am Mon–Sat ▪ MC, V accepted ▪ Dh Dh

This hip bar-restaurant wouldn't look out of place in Paris *(see p56)*.

6 L'Annexe
MAP B4 ▪ 4 rue Moulay Ali, Guéliz ▪ 0524 43 40 10 ▪ Open noon–2:30pm and 7:30–11:30pm daily; closed Sat for lunch and Sun evening Dh Dh

Serving perfectly executed French classics in a stylish modern bistro.

7 Al Fassia
MAP B5 ▪ 55 blvd Mohammed Zerktouni ▪ 0524 43 40 60 ▪ Open noon–2:30pm, 7:30–11pm Wed–Mon ▪ Credit cards accepted ▪ Dh Dh

This is an excellent frill-free restaurant with a lovely, peaceful garden *(see p60)*.

8 Le Catanzaro
MAP B5 ▪ 42 rue Tarik Bnou Ziad, Guéliz ▪ 0524 43 37 31 ▪ Open noon–2:30pm and 7:15–11pm Mon–Sat ▪ Credit cards accepted ▪ Dh

Reliable French/Italian restaurant serving pizzas, pastas and steaks.

9 Café Les Négociants
MAP B5 ▪ Cnr ave Mohammed V & blvd Mohammed Zerktouni ▪ 0615 14 54 17 ▪ Open 7am–11pm daily ▪ No credit cards ▪ Dh

Stop at this popular café for strong, tar-like coffee.

10 Comptoir Darna
MAP C6 ▪ Ave Echouhada ▪ 0524 43 77 02 ▪ Open 8pm–1am daily ▪ MC, V accepted ▪ Dh Dh

As well as the good food, Comptoir Darna is a great night out *(see p56)*.

Stylish dining room at Kechmara

See map on p78

🔟 Essaouira

Where Marrakech is a uniform pink, this sun-beaten town, two hours and 30 minutes away on Morocco's Atlantic coast, is

a nautical blue and white. The prosperity of the place peaked in the 18th and 19th centuries when it was the most important port on the North African coast. It faded from consciousness in the 20th century, but drew plenty of travelling hippies in the 1960s and early 1970s. Today, its agreeably languid atmosphere is stirred only in late afternoon when the fishing fleet returns. Essaouira is known as the "Windy City" because of the constant winds that blow from the sea.

A cannon on Essaouira's ramparts

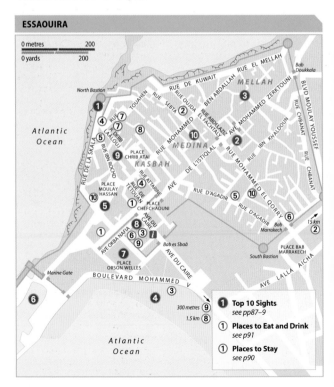

ESSAOUIRA

1 **Top 10 Sights**
see pp87–9

1 **Places to Eat and Drink**
see p91

1 **Places to Stay**
see p90

Previous pages Cacti in the Majorelle Gardens

1 Ramparts
MAP N1

Essaouira's current layout can be traced back to 1765. That year, the town's local ruler captured a French ship and hired one of its passengers, who was an architect, to rebuild his port. He had the city surrounded with a heavy defensive wall, much of which still stands today. The most impressive stretch is the Skala de la Ville, where you can go for a walk along the top of the ramparts and examine several of the ancient cannons in the area.

Street sellers in the Jewish quarter

2 The Souks
MAP P1

At the heart of the medina is a lively market, the Souk Jdid, divided into four quarters by the intersection of two main thoroughfares. There is a daily souk for fish, spice and grains, and a cloistered square, known as the Joutia, where second-hand items are sold at auction.

3 The Mellah
MAP Q1

During the 18th and 19th centuries, a Jewish community gained prominence in Essaouira, becoming the most important economic group. The community has long since left and the town's Jewish quarter, or *mellah*, is in a dilapidated state. Visitors can reach it by following the alleys just inside the ramparts beyond Skala de la Ville. Former Jewish residences are fronted by balconies. In some cases, the Hebrew inscriptions on their lintels are also visible.

4 The Beach
MAP P2

Essaouira's beach, to the south of the medina, is one of the finest in Morocco. However, the strong winds that batter this part of the Atlantic coast can make it a little cold – not that this bothers the windsurfers or the boys who play football here.

5 Place Moulay Hassan
MAP N2

Place Moulay Hassan is the focal point of Essaouira. A square in two parts, narrow and elongated to the north and opening out at the southern end, it lies between the medina proper and the port, and everybody passes through it at some point. It is lined by small cafés where locals spend their time.

Ceramics for sale in the souk

Small fishing boats moored below the fortress guarding Essaouira's port

6 The Port
MAP N2

Guarded by a small square fortress, Essaouira's port, the Skala du Port, is still a working concern complete with a boat yard. Even today, vessels are constructed out of wood. A daily market kicks into life between 3 and 5pm with the arrival of the day's catch. Visitors can watch as the fish are auctioned off and sample the fresh produce by indulging in the sardines that are grilled to order at the port end of place Moulay Hassan.

7 Place Orson Welles
MAP N2–P2

Between the medina walls and the beach is a small park-like square named place Orson Welles, in honour of the great film-maker who travelled to Essaouira in 1949 to shoot his version of *Othello*. Since then, Essaouira and the surrounding area have been used as movie locations in many international film

Bust of the director in place Orson Welles

projects, including Oliver Stone's epic *Alexander* and Ridley Scott's *Kingdom of Heaven*.

8 Galerie Damgaard
MAP P2 ■ Ave Okba Bin Nafia, Medina ■ 0524 78 44 46 ■ Open 9am–1pm, 3–7pm daily

For about a quarter of a century a generation of painters and sculptors have made Essaouira an important centre of artistic activity. Many of these artists were brought to public attention by Dane Frederic Damgaard who used to run this influential gallery.

9 Musée Sidi Mohamed Ben Abdellah
MAP N1 ■ Rue derb Laâlouj, Medina ■ 0524 47 53 00 ■ Open 8:30am–6:30pm Wed–Mon

This small ethnographic museum occupies a 19th-century house that was formerly the town hall. It contains displays of ancient crafts, weapons and jewellery. Also displayed here are the musical instruments and accessories that were used by religious brotherhoods. You can also view some stunning examples of traditional Berber and Jewish costumes.

⑩ The Medina
MAP P1

As in Marrakech, Essaouira's medina is a labyrinth of narrow streets. However, it is not as hard to navigate as it is bisected by one long, straight street. This street begins at the port and runs all the way up to the north gate, the Bab Doukkala, undergoing two name changes along the way.

A narrow street of the medina

MUSIC CITY

Essaouira was a popular hippy stop-over in the late 1960s. Jimi Hendrix, famously passed through, as did Frank Zappa. Cat Stevens, now Yusuf Islam, still returns each summer. The hippy influence lingers on: the annual Gnawa Festival d'Essaouira attracts a variety of musicians from around the globe and has been described as the world's biggest jam session.

A DAY BY THE SEA

▶ MORNING

It is possible to do Essaouira as a day trip from Marrakech (although it's worth staying at least a couple of days). You can get an early morning **CTM bus** from gare routière (see p107), a Supratours coach at 8:30am or a grand taxi from a rank behind the bus station and arrive by 10 or 11am. You will probably enter the city from the **Bab Marrakech** and follow rue Mohammed El Qorry to the main crossroads of the medina, which is also the middle of the **souks** (see p87). Walk south down avenue de L'Istiqlal, taking a right turn into shop-lined **rue Attarine**. The first left leads down to **place Moulay Hassan** (see p87), a great place for a drink at one of the many cafés. Follow the road south to the **port** where you can have a lunch of grilled sardines.

AFTERNOON

From the port, backtrack to place Moulay Hassan but take a left at the famed **Taros** café (see p91) and follow the narrow alley, **rue de la Skala**, along the inside of the high sea wall. There are some woodcarving workshops here. After a short walk, head up to the **ramparts** (see p87) for a wonderful view. Descend and then continue to the *mellah* (see p87). Find your way back to the souks and again head along avenue de L'Istiqlal south. Take a left on avenue du Caire, exiting by the **Bab Es Sbaâ** and taking a right for the **beach** (see p87). The Chalet de la Plage is perfect for dinner by the ocean.

See map on p86 ◀

Places to Stay

A peaceful and verdant courtyard at boutique hotel Villa Maroc

1 Villa Maroc
MAP P2 ▪ 10 rue Abdellah Ben Yassine ▪ 0524 47 31 47 ▪ www.villa-maroc.com ▪ ⑩⑩

Essaouira's first boutique hotel was built by combining four houses. It has fine views from the roof terraces.

2 Riad Dar Maya
MAP P1 ▪ Rue d'Oujda ▪ 0524 78 56 87 ▪ www.riaddarmaya.com ▪ ⑩⑩

A five-room, English-owned boutique riad with a heated rooftop plunge pool; it also has a pretty *hammam*.

3 Palazzo Desdemona
MAP P2 ▪ 12–14 rue Youssef El Fassi ▪ 0524 47 22 27 ▪ www.palazzodesdemona.com ▪ ⑩

Room sizes vary but it has plenty of atmosphere and is excellent value.

4 Riad Al Madina
MAP P2 ▪ 9 rue Attarine ▪ 0524 47 59 07 ▪ www.riadalmadina.com ▪ ⑩

This former hippy café, supposedly frequented by Jimi Hendrix, has been restored as a charming riad.

5 Riad Nakhla
MAP P2 ▪ 12 rue d'Agadir ▪ 0524 47 49 40 ▪ www.riadnakhla.com ▪ ⑩

All rooms have en-suite bathrooms; there's a courtyard with a fountain and a terrific roof terrace.

6 L'Heure Bleue
MAP Q2 ▪ 2 rue Ibn Batouta ▪ 0524 78 34 34 ▪ www.heure-bleue.com ▪ ⑩⑩⑩⑩

This Relais & Chateaux member has luxe rooms, a rooftop pool and a spa, and offers superb fine dining.

7 Dar Adul
MAP N1 ▪ 63 rue Touahen ▪ 0524 47 39 10 ▪ www.dar-adul.com ▪ ⑩

A cosy house with seven bedrooms, a sitting room and a roof terrace.

8 Riad Malaïka
MAP P1 ▪ Rue Zayan ▪ 0524 78 49 08 ▪ www.riad-essaouira-malaika.com ▪ ⑩

Beautifully preserved 300-year-old riad. Rooms are small but nicely decorated. It also has a roof terrace.

9 Madada Mogador
MAP P2 ▪ Rue Youssef El Fassi ▪ 0524 47 55 12 ▪ www.madada.com ▪ ⑩⑩

Perfectly located overlooking place Orson Welles and the beach; with spacious rooms and a roof terrace.

10 Lalla Mira
MAP Q2 ▪ 14 rue d'Algérie ▪ 0524 47 50 46 ▪ www.lallamirableue.com ▪ ⑩

This eco-hotel has a farm and an organic restaurant. Guests can use the *hammam* next door.

 See map on p86

Places to Eat

PRICE CATEGORIES
For a full meal for one with half a bottle of wine (or equivalent meal), plus taxes and extra charges.
Ⓓ under 200 Dh ⒹⒹ 200–400 Dh
ⒹⒹⒹ over 400 Dh

Port-Side Fish Stalls
MAP N2 ▪ Place Moulay Hassan
▪ Ⓓ

The best meal in Essaouira is seafood fresh off the boat, grilled and eaten at a group of stalls on the port side of place Moulay Hassan.

2 La Fromagerie
Douar Larabe, Route Côtière de Safi ▪ 0666 23 35 34 ▪ Open noon–midnight daily ▪ ⒹⒹ

A small hillside restaurant just a ten-minute taxi ride from the medina. Each dish involves cheese and is made on the premises.

3 Le Chalet de la Plage
MAP P3 ▪ Blvd Mohammed V ▪ 0524 47 59 72 ▪ Open 7:30am–11pm daily ▪ ⒹⒹ

Enjoy the superb beachfront setting that matches the quality of fresh fish and seafood.

4 Les Alizés Mogador
MAP N1 ▪ 26 rue de la Skala ▪ 0524 47 68 19 ▪ Open noon–3:30pm, 7:30–11pm daily ▪ Ⓓ

This restaurant serves hearty portions of Moroccan food.

5 Umia
MAP N2 ▪ 22 rue de la Skala ▪ 0524 78 33 95 ▪ Open 1–3pm, 7–9:30pm daily ▪ ⒹⒹ

Sample lobster ravioli and chocolate fondant at this French restaurant.

6 La Table Madada
MAP P2 ▪ Rue Youssef El Fassi ▪ 0524 47 55 12 ▪ Open 7–10pm Wed–Mon ▪ ⒹⒹ

The Madada riad is one of the cosiest spots in town. The contemporary Moroccan menu focuses on fresh fish and Atlantic seafood alongside produce from the market.

7 Triskala Café
MAP N1 ▪ Rue Touahen ▪ 0634 11 84 90 ▪ Open 6:30–10pm Mon–Sat ▪ Ⓓ

A daily-changing menu of fresh fish, vegetarian and vegan dishes served in cave-like rooms just inside the city's seafront ramparts.

8 Zahra's Grill
MAP N2 ▪ Rue Amira Lalla Meriem ▪ 0524 47 48 22 ▪ Open 1–3pm, 7–9:30pm daily; closed mid-Nov–mid-Mar ▪ ⒹⒹ

Expect fabulous seafood, from the octopus salad to the lobster risotto.

9 Côté Plage
MAP Q3 ▪ Blvd Mohammed V ▪ 0524 47 90 00 ▪ ⒹⒹ

Part of the MBeach Sofitel complex, this beachfront café serves tapas and flavoursome barbecued meats.

10 Taros
MAP N2 ▪ Place Moulay Hassan ▪ 0524 47 64 07 ▪ Open 10am–midnight Mon–Sat ▪ Credit cards accepted ▪ ⒹⒹ

Sip a drink on the terrace at sunset, staring out to sea, then enjoy the mix of Moroccan and French dishes. There is live music here most nights.

Taros roof terrace

🔟 Tizi-n-Test Pass

The high-altitude Tizi-n-Test Pass, the more westerly of the two great passes over the Atlas Mountains, is cautiously navigated by the R203 highway to Taroudant. Although the distance between the two cities is only 223 km (138 miles), the road's tortuous hairpins demand so much respect from drivers that the journey takes nearly five hours – not including time to stop off and take in the views along the way. Travellers without their own vehicle or *grand taxi* can make the trip by public transport: southbound buses depart Marrakech each morning. Visitors can also save time by changing buses in Agadir.

The roofless arches of Tin Mal

TIZI-N-TEST PASS

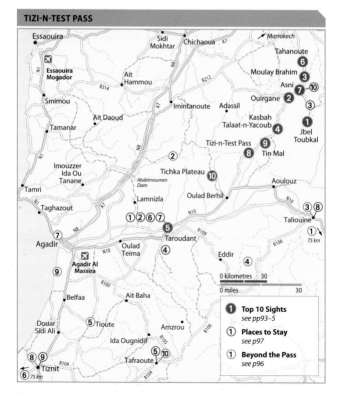

1 Top 10 Sights
see pp93–5

1 Places to Stay
see p97

1 Beyond the Pass
see p96

Snow capped Jbel Toubkal towering over palm trees in the valley below

 Jbel Toubkal
MAP C2 ▪ Bureau des guides:
tel 0524 48 56 26

Take the left fork at Asni to Imlil at the foot of Jbel Toubkal, North Africa's highest peak. Mountain guides can be hired in the centre of Imlil at the *bureau des guides*. The Kasbah du Toubkal, just up the hill, is a good place to stay *(see p97)*.

 Ouirgane
MAP C2

A pretty little village 16 km (10 miles) south of Asni, Ouirgane is hidden among the tree-lined valley above the Oued Nifis river. Here, there is a shrine to a Jewish saint as well as two salt factories (one modern, one traditional). The village is a great base for hiking, mountain biking or horse-riding excursions into the Atlas Mountains.

3 Moulay Brahim
MAP C2

South of Tahanoute, the road winds uphill to Moulay Brahim, named after a local saint. There is a green-roofed shrine dedicated to him in the middle of the village which non-Muslims are forbidden to enter.

4 Kasbah Talaat-n-Yacoub
MAP C2

South of Ouirgane, the road climbs steadily through a bare and rocky landscape. After you pass through the small Berber hamlet of Ijoujak, the hilltop fortress of Kasbah Talaat-n-Yacoub is visible to the right. This was once a stronghold of the Goundafi tribe who controlled access to the Tizi-n-Test pass until the early 20th century, when they were subdued by the French.

 Taroudant
MAP B2

Built on the proceeds of gold brought from the Sahara, Taroudant was the capital of the Saadian dynasty in the early 16th century. Today, enclosed within reddish-yellow walls, the city resembles a smaller, sleepier version of Marrakech. It features a grand kasbah that can be reached by passing under the triple-arched Saadian Gates, as well as some foul-smelling tanneries. You will also find two excellent souks in Taroudant.

A souk in the city of Taroudant

Country market at Tahanoute

6 Tahanoute
MAP C1

The administrative centre of Tahanoute is just a 20-minute drive south of Marrakech. The old village has a cascade of red clay houses that surround a massive rock sheltering the shrine of Sidi Mohammed El Kebir, whose festival is celebrated at Mouloud – the birthday of the Prophet Mohammed. This was the subject of Winston Churchill's last painting in 1958. A market is held here every Tuesday.

7 Asni
MAP C2

The village of Asni lies at a fork in the road – a left turn leads up to the village of Imlil and the striking kasbahs of Tamadot (see p97) and Toubkal (see p63). Jbel Toubkal dominates the view to the west, but there is little for visitors to explore at Asni itself, apart from shops selling trinkets (although these are cheaper in Marrakech). The highlight here is the busy country market held on Saturdays – one of the largest in the Atlas Mountains.

8 Tizi-n-Test Pass
MAP B2

How much travellers enjoy the experience of this 2,092-m (6,861-ft) pass depends on whether they are a passenger or in the driver's seat. Drivers have to keep their eyes glued to the road ahead in order to negotiate the endless hairpin bends. The narrow road, with no safety barriers, means there aren't many opportunities to enjoy the beautiful views. But for those in the passenger seat, the vistas across the plains of the Sous to the south are spectacular. There are various souvenir stalls and small cafés located on the pass itself, where drivers and passengers can stop and take in the scenery.

9 Tin Mal
MAP C2 ■ **Closed Fridays** ■ **Adm**

The main attraction at Tin Mal is an ancient mosque that dates back to the time of the Almohads (see p38). Back in the 12th century, this was the heart of a mountain empire that

The hillside town of Asni

ARGAN OIL

The precious argan trees, similar in appearance to olive trees, are found only in southwest Morocco. They bear a fruit from which oil can be extracted by splitting, roasting and pressing the nuts. Locals use it as a medicine; it is also a staple of beauty and massage treatments, and tastes delicious when drizzled on couscous.

unified local tribes under a militant version of Islam. It was from here that an army set out in 1144 to lay siege to Marrakech and went on to conquer the rest of Morocco. The restored mosque provided the basic architectural prototype for the impressive Koutoubia in Marrakech. Though roofless, it continues to be the venue for Friday prayers – the only day that it is inaccessible to non-Muslim visitors.

⑩ Tichka Plateau
MAP B2

Set among beautiful meadows, the Tichka Plateau is found to the north of Taroudant. Particularly striking in spring, when the wild flowers are in full bloom, it is a fine place to go trekking, but is best enjoyed with qualified guides. Go to the *bureau des guides* in Imlil *(see p93)* to arrange a guided trek.

A DAY IN TAROUDANT

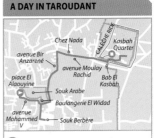

▶ **MORNING**

Although **Taroudant** resembles a more ramshackle Marrakech at first sight, it has more of an African identity than an Arab one. Unlike most other Moroccan cities, it was never occupied by the French and consequently it does not possess a European quarter. Begin your exploration of the city on **place El Alaouyine**, known by its Berber name of place Assarag. Walk down **avenue Mohammed V,** south of the square, and head east into **Souk Arabe**, famed for its antique shops. At the souk's edge, **Boulangerie El Widad** offers tasty Moroccan pastries. South of the main street and across place El Nasr is **Souk Berbère**, the main fruit and vegetable market. Return north up avenue Bir Anzarené and take a right on avenue Moulay Rachid; sample the tajines at **Chez Nada**.

AFTERNOON

As you walk east on avenue Moulay Rachid along a path lined with orange trees, you will come upon the triple-arched Saadian Gates at **Bab El Kasbah**. These lead to the walled **kasbah quarter** built by Mohammed ech-Cheikh, who made it the capital of the Saadian empire. The poorest part of town, it used to house the governor's palace. Stop for a snack at one of the local cafés and then make your way back to the Bab El Kasbah. Hop into a waiting *calèche* and, for a small fee, do a circuit of the city walls. You can take the *calèche* back to place El Alaouyine.

See map on p92

Beyond the Pass

 Taznakht
MAP C2
Famed for the carpets woven by the Ouaouzgite tribe, the town of Taznakht sits beneath Jbel Siroua.

2 The Atlas Mountains
MAP B2
The peaks of the western High Atlas – particularly 3,555-m (11,667-ft) high Jbel Aoulime – can be reached by road north of Taroudant.

3 Taliouine
MAP C2
Taliouine, a town with a ruined kasbah once owned by the Glaoui clan *(see pp39 & 100)*, is also one of the world's biggest saffron growing areas.

4 The Anti-Atlas
MAP C3
As the R106 from Taliouine crosses the Anti-Atlas at the 94-km (58-mile) mark, you'll find Igherm – a large mountain village where women wear black with coloured headbands.

The impressive Tioute Kasbah

5 Tioute Kasbah
MAP B3
About 37 km (23 miles) southeast of Taroudant, the imposing Tioute Kasbah (containing a restaurant) dominates a palm grove. This was the location for the film *Ali Baba and the Forty Thieves* in 1954.

A colourful building in Sidi Ifni

6 Sidi Ifni
This colonial-style town sits on the crest of a rocky plateau overlooking the Atlantic. To get here, follow the coast road after Tiznit.

7 Agadir
MAP A3 ■ Tourist information: ave du Prince Moulay Abdallah ■ 0528 84 63 77
Flattened by an earthquake in 1960, Agadir was rebuilt and is now a thriving charter tourist resort. The grim aspect of the town is somewhat offset by its fantastic beaches.

8 Tiznit
MAP A3
In this small town, surrounded by pink *pisé* ramparts, visitors feel the proximity of both the Atlantic and the desert. Its central *méchouar* parade ground is lined with cafés and shops.

9 Sous Massa National Park
MAP A3
The park along the banks of Wadi Massa contains reed beds inhabited by large flocks of flamingoes and the endangered northern bald ibis.

10 Tafraoute
MAP B3
At an altitude of 1,200 m (3,938 ft), Tafraoute stands in the heart of a stunning valley in the Anti-Atlas. The palm groves here are lush and when they flower in February, the almond trees are covered with clouds of dusky pink and white blossom.

→ *See map on p92*

Places to Stay

PRICE CATEGORIES
For a standard double room per night
with taxes and breakfast if included.
....
 Dh under 1,200 Dh DhDh 1,200–2,500 Dh
DhDhDh over 2,500 Dh

1 Le Palais Oumensour
MAP B2 ▪ Burj Al Mansour
Oumensour Tadjount, Taroudant
▪ 0528 55 02 15 ▪ www.palaisoumen
sour.com ▪ No credit cards ▪ Dh
Well located for those who wish to
explore Taroudant on foot, this hotel
has stylish, comfortable rooms.

2 Hotel Dar Zitoune
MAP B2 ▪ Boutarial El Barrania,
Taroudant ▪ 0528 55 11 42 ▪ www.
darzitoune.com ▪ DhDh
Set out like a Berber village, this riad
features a large pool and offers various
suites, bungalows and tented rooms.

3 Kasbah du Toubkal
MAP C2 ▪ BP31, Imlil ▪ 0524 48
56 11 ▪ www.kasbahdutoubkal.com
▪ Dh
This beautifully restored kasbah is
a great base for trekking (see p63).

4 Riad Ain Khadra
MAP B2 ▪ Route d'Agadir,
Taroudant ▪ 0528 85 41 42 ▪ No credit
cards ▪ www.riad-ain-khadra.com ▪ Dh
The French owners of this charming
maison d'hôtes have five traditional
rooms and three suites arranged
around a courtyard pool.

5 L'Arganier d'Ammelne
MAP B3 ▪ Route d'Agadir,
Tafraoute ▪ 0661 92 60
64 ▪ www.arganier
ammelne.jimdo.com ▪ Dh
A few minutes' drive from
central Tafraout, this
basic but comfortable
option has air-
conditioned en-suite
rooms, a garden and
a terrace. It also offers
camping options.

6 Villa Talaa
MAP B2 ▪ Taroudant ▪ 0621 70
20 90 ▪ www.villa-talaa.com ▪ Dh
About a ten-minute drive from
Taroudant is this peaceful hotel with
11 rooms. All have patios opening
onto the garden and the pool.

7 Dar Fatima
MAP B2 ▪ Tasoukt Tighzifn,
Taroudant ▪ 0662 29 75 75 ▪ www.
darfatima.com ▪ Dh
Right in the centre of town, this
simple yet friendly riad has great
views from its rooftop terrace.

8 Escale Rando Taliouine
MAP C2 ▪ Taliouine ▪ 0528 53
46 00 ▪ www.escalerando.com ▪ Dh
This sparse but functional hotel
occupies part of an old kasbah.
The hospitable owners are happy
to arrange treks and tours.

9 Hotel Idou Tiznit
MAP A3 ▪ Ave Hassan II, Tiznit
▪ 0528 60 03 33 ▪ Credit cards
accepted ▪ Dh
Notable for its location rather than its
decor, this hotel is a good option for
those travelling on a limited budget.

10 Kasbah Tamadot
MAP C2 ▪ BP67, Asni ▪ 0524 36
82 00 ▪ www.virginlimitededition.
com/kasbah-tamadot ▪ DhDhDh
Owned by Richard Branson, this
expensive retreat is located in a
tranquil spot at the foothills of the
Atlas Mountains.

A suite at Kasbah Tamadot

TOP 10 Tizi-n-Tichka Pass

Saharan camel

The N9 highway runs southeast from Marrakech over the Atlas Mountains, crossing the country's highest pass. On the other side, it then descends to the town of Ouarzazate, considered the gateway to the Sahara. Along the way, travellers will come across some interesting sights, including the kasbahs of Telouet and Aït Benhaddou (both off the main road). From start to finish, the route is 196 km (122 miles) on a good road. There are some stretches that demand careful driving; as a result, the journey can take nearly four hours. Travellers can arrange for a *grand taxi* or hire a car. Alternatively, several buses travel this route daily from Marrakech's bus station. Transport company Supratours also runs daily trips to Ouarzazate.

1 Aït Ourir
MAP C1

This busy little rural town 35 km (22 miles) outside Marrakech becomes even more active on Fridays, when farmers trade camels, sheep and other agricultural produce in a weekly country market. If visitors pass through on the right day, it makes for a great hour-long stop off.

2 Kasbah Taourirt
MAP D2 ▪ Open 8am–6:30pm daily ▪ Adm

The main landmark of Ouarzazate, this large kasbah used to belong to the Glaoui tribe. Parts are still inhabited, while other sections have been carefully restored. Its atmospheric, narrow alleys evoke a sense of what life here was like in the 19th century.

TIZI-N-TICHKA PASS

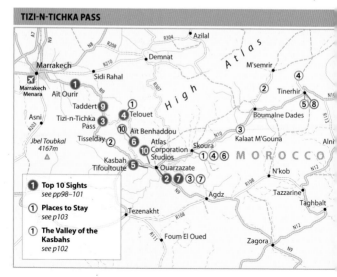

1 **Top 10 Sights**
see pp98–101

1 **Places to Stay**
see p103

1 **The Valley of the Kasbahs**
see p102

The winding road that cuts through the Tizi-n-Tichka Pass

③ Tizi-n-Tichka Pass
MAP C2

As the road leaves Taddert, the green landscape turns scenically rugged and barren – the twisting, precipitous drops keeping drivers focused. At its highest point, the pass peaks at 2,260 m (7,415 ft), marked by no more than a few stalls selling colourful rocks found in the region. While some of these rocks are fake, the real ones reveal glittering crystal formations when broken.

④ Kasbah Telouet
MAP C2 ▪ Adm

Telouet, the stronghold of the Glaoui tribe (see p100), who, in the early 20th century, came to rule all of southern Morocco under French sponsorship, is a village dominated by a magnificent kasbah. Abandoned for nearly half a century, much of the structure is crumbling and dangerous. However, travellers can visit the ornate reception hall and its rooftop terrace, which affords stunning views.

⑤ Kasbah Tifoultoute
MAP D2 ▪ Open 8am–5pm daily

Tifoultoute is another kasbah that once belonged to the Glaoui, and is situated just outside of Ouarzazate. Although parts of it are crumbling away, one section has been rebuilt and serves as a hotel and restaurant. The location is beautiful.

Kasbah Tifoultoute in the Atlas Mountains

THAMI EL GLAOUI

In 1893, the Glaoui tribe of Telouet was rewarded for rescuing Sultan Moulay Hassan and his army from a raging blizzard. They benefited further after the French took over – Thami El Glaoui was made *pasha* (lord) and became one of the most powerful men in the country. Hated for his support of the French, he died soon after Morocco gained independence in 1956.

The town of Ouarzazate

6 Aït Benhaddou
MAP D2

This sprawling kasbah features on UNESCO's list of World Heritage Sites and is one of the best pre-served in the region. It is also among the most famous, and, thanks to its popularity with visiting film producers and directors, it has been immortalized in dozens of Hollywood movies, including *Lawrence of Arabia*, *The Last Temptation of Christ*, *The Mummy*, *Gladiator* and *Alexander*. Part of its appeal lies in its location, with the kasbah tumbling down a hillside beside the Ouarzazate River. It is still partially inhabited by ten families.

7 Ouarzazate
MAP D2 ■ Tourist Office: 0524 88 23 66

The so-called "Gateway to the Sahara" (pronounced "war-zazat") is a town of around 60,000 people. Most visitors tend to spend at least one night here before pushing on south to the desert proper, or heading east to the Dadès Gorge and beyond *(see p102)*. The number of hotels in town is always increasing and the quality is constantly improving. There are plenty of interesting activities in the area: from camel-trekking and quad biking to desert safaris and guided tours of the Atlas film studios for which the town is renowned.

Aït Benhaddou

8 Valley of the Kasbahs

From Ouarzazate, visitors can continue east through the Skoura Valley along a road dotted with oases and the ancient mud-brick strongholds that give the route its more romantic nickname *(see p102)*. The road eventually runs out at Merzouga, 350 miles (562 km) from Marrakech, and there is nothing to be found between here and the Algerian border but sand dunes.

9 Taddert
MAP C1

After Aït Ourir, the last stop before the pass is the busy village of Taddert. In the higher part of the settlement, a handful of good cafés offer views of the valley below. When the pass is closed by bad weather, a barrier is lowered to halt all traffic.

View of the valley below Taddert

10 Atlas Corporation Studios
MAP D2 ■ 0524 88 22 12
■ Open Oct–Feb: 8:15am–5:15pm;
Mar–Sep: 8:15am–6:45pm
■ Guided tours last 30–40 mins
■ Adm ■ www.studiosatlas.com

Ouarzazate has become the centre of the Moroccan film industry and is home to the Atlas Corporation Studios. Found 6 km (4 miles) to the north of town, the studios were built to provide infrastructure, sound stages and sets for movies; films shot here include *Gladiator* and *Kingdom of Heaven*. Film buffs can see sets here such as the Egyptian temple from the French production of *Asterix and Cleopatra*. A shuttle bus runs between the studio and avenue Mohammed V.

SOUTH TO THE DESERT

▶ DAY ONE

From **Ouarzazate**, the road continues south through the **Drâa Valley** down to the administrative town of **Zagora**. After a drive of about four hours, stop at **Tamnougalt**, a dramatic *ksar* (fortified village) 10 minutes off the main road, 5 km (3 miles) after the small market town of Agdz. Further south is **Kasbah Timiderte**, a fortress from the Glaoui era. Zagora itself is dominated by **Jbel Zagora**, a rocky outcrop at the town's end. The lively market, held on Wednesdays and Sundays, teems with dates that grow in abundance here. Just south of the centre is the pretty hamlet of **Amezrou**. Nearby, the **Kasbah des Juifs** is inhabited by Berber silversmiths (the Jews who once lived here are long gone). Zagora's most famous attraction is at the town's exit – a sign with a camel caravan that reads "Timbuktu, 52 Days".

DAY TWO

The village of **M'Hamid** is 96 km (60 miles) further south of Zagora. En route, **Tamegroute's** mosque-and-shrine complex is off limits to non-Muslims, except for the library with its collection of ancient manuscripts. Drive 5 km (3 miles) further on and you will see the first of the sand dunes at **Tinfou**. The best dunes can be accessed from M'Hamid, a sleepy outpost at the road's end – a one-street settlement that feels like it is at the end of the world. Desert trips, from excursions of a few hours, to expeditions lasting several days, can be arranged.

See map on pp98–9

The Valley of the Kasbahs

 Skoura
MAP D2

The first town east of Ouarzazate is notable for a *palmeraie* with impressive old kasbahs including the Kasbah Amridil (part hotel, part museum), once owned by the Glaoui family (*see p100*).

Kasbah Amridil, near Skoura

 Dadès Gorge
MAP E1

Follow the road north from Boumalne Dades to this incredible gorge, a spectacular backdrop for several kasbahs.

 Kalaat M'Gouna
MAP D2

This small town lies at the heart of rose-growing country. Most of the petals picked each spring are exported around the world for use in the perfume industry.

Todra Gorge
MAP E1

Sheer cliffs rise from this narrow gorge with Tamtattouchte village at the northern end. Two hotels make an overnight stay possible.

Erg Chebbi dunes, Merzouga

 Tinerhir
MAP E1 ■ Tourist information: Hotel Tomboctou; 0524 83 51 91

The region's administrative centre is bordered by lush palm groves. Known for its silver jewellery, it has several working silver mines nearby.

 Goulmima
MAP E1

The fortified villages, or *ksours*, here were built to defend against the pillaging nomads. A walled town east of the Erfoud road is worth a detour.

 Errachidia
MAP F1 ■ Tourist information: 0535 57 09 44

From this town, known for its pottery and carved wooden objects, the palm groves of Ziz and Tafilalt begin.

 Erfoud
MAP F1

This town serves as a base for tours to the Erg Chebbi sand dunes and the Tafilalt palm grove. It also hosts a three-day Date Festival each October following the date harvest.

 Rissani
MAP F1

This ancient town dating back to the 7th century lies on the edge of the Sahara and has a very famous souk.

 Merzouga
MAP F2

A Saharan oasis at the foot of the Erg Chebbi dunes, from where camel drivers offer desert tours.

Places to Stay

PRICE CATEGORIES
For a standard double room per night
with taxes and breakfast if included.

Dh under 1,200 Dh　Dh Dh 1,200–2,500 Dh
Dh Dh Dh over 2,500 Dh

1 Auberge Telouet
MAP C2 ▪ Telouet ▪ 0524 89
07 17 ▪ www.telouet.com ▪ No credit
cards ▪ Dh
A lovely budget auberge in the
traditional style. The walls are made
of huge stones, and rooms are
spartan but attractive. Not all
rooms have en-suite facilities.

2 Irocha
MAP C2 ▪ Tisselday ▪ 0667 73
70 02 ▪ www.irocha.com ▪ No credit
cards ▪ Dh
Midway between Telouet and Aït
Benhaddou, this hotel has plenty of
charming touches, such as multiple
terraces and gardens. It also has a
pool and a *hammam*.

3 Le Berbère Palace
MAP D2 ▪ Quartier Mansour
Eddahabi Ouarzazate ▪ 0524 88 31 05
▪ www.hotel-berberepalace.com
▪ Dh Dh
One of the three luxury hotels in
Ouarzazate, it has air-conditioned
bungalows, a large pool, a *hammam*,
a solarium and tennis courts.

4 Kasbah Aït Ben Moro
MAP D2 ▪ Skoura ▪ 0524 85 21
16 ▪ www.kasbahaitbenmoro.com
▪ No credit cards ▪ Dh
At night, this 18th-century fortress
with thick walls and a palm-tree
garden is lit by lanterns, creating
a cosy atmosphere.

5 Riad Salam
MAP F1 ▪ Route de Rissani,
Erfoud ▪ 0535 57 66 65 ▪ Dh
While this is a budget option, it has
plenty to offer, including a swimming
pool, perfect for a refreshing dip, as
well as a popular bar.

6 Dar Ahlam
MAP D2 ▪ Douar Oulad,
Chakh Ali, Skoura ▪ 0524 85 22 39
▪ www.darahlam.com ▪ Dh Dh Dh
A kasbah-turned-luxury-boutique
hotel with a *hammam* and use of a
four-wheel-drive car.

7 Dar Daïf
MAP D2 ▪ Route de Zagora,
Ouarzazate ▪ 0524 85 49 47
▪ www.dardaif.ma ▪ Dh
This 14-room guesthouse has a
hammam, a pool and a bedroom
equipped for disabled guests.

Dar Daïf's courtyard and pool

8 Kasbah Lamrani
MAP E1 ▪ Zone Touristique, blvd
Mohammed V, Tinerhir ▪ 0524 83 50
17 ▪ www.kasbahlamrani.com ▪ Dh
This small kasbah, with a pool, is
a good base for a trip to the
Todra Gorge.

9 Kasbah Xaluca
MAP F1 ▪ Erfoud ▪ 0535 57 84
50 ▪ www.xaluca.com ▪ Dh
A large place with a big swimming
pool, this is tailored to suit groups.

10 La Rose du Sable
MAP D2 ▪ Aït Benhaddou
▪ 0524 89 00 22 ▪ www.larose
dusable.com ▪ Dh
Very comfortable, family-friendly
hotel with a courtyard swimming
pool and great views of the kasbah.

See map on pp98–9

Streetsmart

Moroccan spices in colourful tajines at the Spice Market

Getting to and Around Marrakech

Arriving by Air

Marrakech is most easily accessible by air, which is how the majority of visitors arrive. **Royal Air Maroc** is the national airline, with regular international services. The cheapest flights tend to be those operated by the budget companies **easyJet**, **Ryanair** and **Norwegian**.

Marrakech is served by **Marrakech Airport** (RAK), which is just 3 miles (5 km) from the Medina. Many major European airlines, as well as **Etihad** and **Qatar Airways**, fly direct to Marrakech; other international airlines may fly into Casablanca, requiring a change of carrier, or require connections via a European hub, such as Paris or Madrid.

On arrival you need to complete an embarkation card before passport control. Once you have collected your luggage, taxis can be found outside the arrivals hall. Prices for airport taxis are massively inflated. There is a board showing prices to the various parts of Marrakech; however, the drivers do not usually follow it. It is best to agree a price with your driver before setting off. For Jemaa el Fna or Guéliz you should not pay more than 150 Dh.

There is also a bus (No.19), which departs every 20–30 minutes and which runs to Jemaa el Fna via all the large hotels; it costs 30 Dh, or 50 Dh return.

Arriving by Train

Train services from Casablanca, Fès, Rabat and Tangier arrive at Marrakech's impressive **ONCF Railway Station**, which is located on the western edge of the new city. It has the city's only free public toilets, as well as Western fast-food outlets. From the station it is a short walk into central Guéliz, or a ten-minute taxi ride to Jemaa el Fna for the Medina, which should cost no more than 50 Dh.

Arriving by Bus

Both the national bus company, **CTM**, and the biggest private bus company, **Supratours**, run buses to and from Marrakech and other major Moroccan destinations. The CTM station is just south of the train station, while the Supratours ticket office is at the train station.

Getting Around on Foot

Marrakech is small and the best way to get around is on foot. In fact, in the Medina you have no choice, as Jemaa el Fna and many other areas are off limits to cars. This does not, however, prevent the large number of scooters and bicycles that career through the alleys, ignoring the signs forbidding such vehicles. The network of streets is labyrinthine and street signs are few so expect to get lost a lot. When you do, do not panic, because you will never be more than a few minutes' walk from somewhere familiar.

The walk to the new town of Guéliz, beyond the old city walls, takes about 20 minutes. You will want to do it once, but for a second visit, you may like to take a taxi.

Getting Around by Taxi

Everybody, Moroccans included, gets around by taxi. There are two types: *grands taxis* and *petits taxis*. The former, which tend to be big Peugeots or Mercedes, are used for long-distance journeys (and the airport run) and operate like minibuses, collecting multiple passengers going to various destinations but all generally in the same direction. Most visitors are unlikely to use them.

What you will use a lot of are the *petits taxis*, which are standard beige-coloured cars used for short-distance journeys and carrying a maximum of three passengers. Annoyingly these are not metered. You are expected to know in advance how much your journey will cost; if you don't and you have to ask the driver "How much?", you will be overcharged.

Ask a member of staff at your hotel for advice before setting out.

Getting Around by Calèche

A *calèche* is a horse-drawn carriage and they are a frequent sight in Marrakech. They are used almost exclusively by tourists taking sightseeing trips around the city walls. You can find them just west of Jemaa el Fna on Place foucault. Prices can be found listed on a signboard.

Travelling Outside the City

For excursions outside Marrekech, to Essaouira, day trips in the countryside or further afield over the Atlas Mountains, there are several options. The first is to take a *grand taxi* from the bus station

(gare routière), just south of the train station. These go to Casablanca, Fès and Essaouira, among other places. The fares are fixed; just turn up and take a seat.

Buses are slightly more expensive but more comfortable and they run to a schedule. Supratours services are superior to CTM, but the latter serves more places, including destinations south of the Atlas Mountains.

A popular alternative, particularly if you are a group, is to hire your own car and driver. This gives you complete flexibility. Most hotels can organise this for you. You can also hire a car and drive yourself – several major international car hire companies, such as **Avis**, **Europcar**, **Hertz** and **Sixt**, are represented in Marrakech – but the downside is that if you are driving you don't get

to admire the scenery. Car hire is quite expensive, with local agencies charging around 400 Dh a day.

The Moroccan highway code is similar to that of France, so give way on the right (note that whoever is on a town roundabout has priority). The road signs are in Arabic and French. A four-wheel-drive car is a must for heading south over the Atlas Mountains as roads are often steep and the terrain is rocky.

Tour Packages

Numerous companies offer Morocco packages and most of them include stays in Marrakech. **Best of Morocco** is UK-based; **Marrakesh Voyage** is US-based; **Real Morocco Tours** is a reputable Marrakech-based Berber-run operator with an array of packages.

DIRECTORY

ARRIVING BY AIR
Marrakech Airport
0524 44 79 10
easyJet
easyjet.com
Etihad
etihad.com
Norwegian
norwegian.com
Qatar Airways
qatarairways.com
Royal Air Maroc
royalairmaroc.com
Ryanair
ryanair.com

ARRIVING BY TRAIN
ONCF Railway Station
MAP B5 ■ Avenue Hassan II
0524 44 77 78
oncf.ma

ARRIVING BY BUS
CTM
MAP B5 ■ Boulevard Aboubaker Seddik
0800 09 00 30
ctm.ma
Supratours
MAP B5 ■ Avenue Hassan II
0524 42 17 69
supratours.ma

TRAVELLING OUTSIDE THE CITY
Avis
MAP B5 ■ 137 avenue Mohammed V, Guéliz
0524 43 25 25
Europcar
MAP B4 ■ 63 boulevard Mohammed Zerktouni, Guéliz
0524 43 12 28

Hertz
MAP B4 ■ 154 avenue Mohammed V, Guéliz
0524 43 99 84
Sixt
MAP B5 ■ 9 boulevard El Mansour Eddahbi, Guéliz
0522 53 66 15

TOUR PACKAGES
Best of Morocco
0667 19 57 83
morocco-travel.com
Marrakesh Voyage
+1 212 925 6151 (US number)
marrakesh-voyage.com
Real Morocco Tours
0666 47 52 13
realmoroccotours.com

Practical Information

Passports and Visas

Citizens of the EU, Switzerland, the United States, Canada, Australia and New Zealand need a valid passport to visit Morocco, but no visa. To be able to stay for up to three months, your passport should be valid for at least six months after your date of arrival. If your time exceeds the three months, then you must get an extension from the central police station.

The UK, US and Canadian diplomatic offices are in the Moroccan capital, Rabat. The **French Consulate** is in Marrakech.

Travel Safety Advice

Visitors can get up-to-date safety information from the **Foreign and Commonwealth Office** in the UK, the **State Department** in the US and the **Department of Foreign Affairs and Trade** in Australia.

Travel Insurance

All visitors should take out an insurance policy before travelling to Marrakech. There are no reciprocal health agreements between Morocco and the EU countries, and if you fall ill you will have to pay the doctor's bills.

Health

No vaccinations are required for visitors entering Morocco, except for those coming from a country where yellow fever exists. However, vaccinations against hepatitis A and B and typhoid are advised.

Pack a small first-aid kit. To prevent sunstroke wear a hat, use a high factor sunblock and drink lots of water.

In the case of an emergency don't wait for an ambulance: flag a taxi and go to the **Polyclinique du Sud** in the New City, a private hospital with the best treatment. Avoid the under-funded public hospitals.

Pharmacies such as **Pharmacie Centrale** and **Pharmacie du Progrès** are denoted by a green crescent sign and have well-informed staff, who often speak English. British proprietary drugs may not be available.

Personal Security

Violence is rare, though bag snatching and other such opportunistic crimes have been on the rise with the influx of rich foreigners. Be careful when walking through a quiet Medina late in the evening. Pickpockets are also common in the souks and on Jemaa el Fna, so be vigilant.

In case of problems, try the tourist police – the **Brigade Touristique** – at Sidi Mimoun, to the west of Jemaa el Fna (not to be confused with the Judicial Police to the east of Jemaa el Fna), or call the **emergency numbers** (these work throughout Morocco). The main police station is on rue Ibn Hanbal near Jnane El Harti in the New City.

Islam

Islam is the state religion and the king of Morocco is the leader of the faithful. It is therefore considered in bad taste to criticize religion. Dress properly *(see below)* and refrain from overt signs of affection in public.

During the fast of Ramadan, do not eat, drink or smoke in public during the day. Alcohol is frowned upon by Islam. Some Moroccans do drink but they do so discreetly and out of the gaze of the general public. Alcohol is forbidden within the Medina, given the holy status conferred on it courtesy of its seven shrines. However, hotels and restaurants with a predominantly foreign clientele are allowed some flexibility. Non-Muslims are not allowed inside mosques and saintly shrines. If in doubt, ask for advice.

Dress

Although Moroccan women do wear Western clothes, play it safe and dress conservatively. Headscarves are not necessary but neither women nor men should wear shorts. Women should also avoid mini skirts, baring their midriff or leaving their shoulders bare. Revealing bikini tops should be restricted to the hotel pool.

Female Travellers

Marrakech is safe for solo female travellers, although you should expect to attract more than your fair share of attention wherever you go. However, avoid travelling down south on your own. People are more conservative south of the Atlas Mountains. Here, a woman on her own will draw a lot of unwelcome curiosity.

Currency and Banking

The Moroccan unit of currency is the dirham (Dh), divided into 100 centimes. Centimes are of little value but beggars are grateful for them. The most useful coins are the denominations of 1, 2, 5 and 10 dirhams. Try to have a stock of small change with you, especially when travelling by taxi. Notes are in denominations of 20, 50, 100 and 200 dirhams.

In Marrakech, banks are clustered on rue de Bab Agnaou in the Medina and along avenue Mohammed V in Guéliz. ATMs issue cash in dirhams only.

Credit cards are accepted by most of the high-end hotels, and most restaurants and Western-style shops.

Communications

National operator Maroc-Télécom and rivals Meditél and INWI have arrangements with European networks that allow visitors to use mobiles in Morocco. Calls will, of course, be expensive. If you are visiting for a long period, buy a pre-paid SIM card from any of the operators, with shops just off place du 16 Novembre in the New City. Free Wi-Fi is common throughout Marrakech.

There is a main post office on the south side of Jemaa el Fna, which opens 8am–4:15pm Monday–Friday and 8:30am–noon on Saturday. There is another central post office on place du 16 Novembre in Guéliz, with the same opening times. You can find postcards for sale all over the Medina and most shops that sell them also sell stamps.

Newspapers and magazines in Morocco are in French or Arabic; you can pick them up along rue de Bab Agnaou in the Medina. For imports of international English-language press there are two excellent newsstands on avenue Mohammed V in Guéliz, south of place Abdel Moumen Ben Ali.

Opening Hours

Although a Muslim country, much of Morocco follows a Monday to Friday working week. Business hours for banks are 8:15am–3:45pm Monday to Friday (9:30am–2pm during Ramadan). Shops start their day a bit later but stay open until 8pm or 9pm. On Fridays, shops in the souks shut at lunch.

Language

French and Arabic are the main languages. English is spoken widely by those working in the tourism industry.

Time Difference

Morocco standard time follows Greenwich Mean Time (GMT).

Electrical Appliances

The electric current is 220V/50Hz. Moroccan sockets take European-style two-pin plugs.

Weather

Marrakech is warm all year round, although January and February have rainfall, with the temperatures dropping during the nights. The summer heat is at its most oppressive and fierce in July and August. The best times to visit are March to June and September to December. The peak tourist season is Easter and Christmas/ New Year, so be sure to make reservations well ahead in order to secure a room if you plan to visit during these periods.

Islamic Holidays

The main Islamic holidays follow the lunar calendar. They are Eid El Fitr (4–5 June in 2019, 23–24 May in 2020) and Eid El Adha (11–15 August in 2019, 30 July–3 August in 2020). During this time, the city stays shut for a minimum of two days, so travelling is very difficult. In the holy month of Ramadan (begins 5 May in 2019, 23 April in 2020 and lasts for 30 days) many Muslims fast during the day; due to this, many restaurants and eateries are closed until sundown. Some restaurants, especially those in the Medina, may abstain from serving alcohol during the month of Ramadan.

Travellers with Specific Needs

Wheelchair users will find Marrakech a tricky place to navigate, especially in the Medina where the crowded roads tend to be narrow and in poor

condition. Beyond the large hotels and the railway station, very few buildings are disabled-friendly, though the city's better riads will do their best to accommodate.

Sources of Information

The **Office National Marocain du Tourisme** (ONMT) is on place Abdel Moumen Ben Ali in Guéliz. However, it is not always particularly useful and chances are you will find that the staff at your hotel or riad will be of more help.

Marrakech on a Budget

Marrakech is not an expensive place. There are few attractions that come with an entrance fee: most of the best of what there is to see is free of charge. The Medina is compact and best explored on foot, largely eliminating transport costs. Although you can spend heavily on eating out, it is possible to eat well very cheaply. The temptation is to blow your budget in the glittering allure of the souks. This is hard to resist, but remember to haggle at the souk and you should be able to get away with paying around half of the original quoted price.

Tours and Guides

The **ALSA** public transport system runs a *Bus Touristique* from the tourist office in place Abdel Moumen Ben Ali. This double-decker, open-topped bus follows two

circular routes, taking in the Koutoubia, place des Ferblantiers (for the Badii and Bahia palaces), the Menara and Majorelle Gardens and Palmeraie. Services are every 30 minutes from 9am to 5pm or 6pm, depending on the season. Tickets are valid for either 24 or 48 hours, and cost either 100 Dh or 150 Dh. Ask at the tourist office for up-to-date information.

You may be approached in the Medina by people offering their services as guides. Always decline. Any discount a guide may obtain for you at shops will be negated by his own commission, which the shopkeeper will factor into the price he charges you. If you do feel you would like a guide, ask your hotel to organize an official guide for you. Alternatively try booking with a reputable company such as **Travel Link** or **Marrakech Guided Tours**.

Shopping and Haggling

Haggling is de rigueur in the souks. If you do not haggle, you will pay greatly over the odds. It all revolves around the considerable difference between the price offered by the seller and the price that he will actually accept if pushed. Shop around and get a few different quotes on identical items before the game begins in earnest.

You will invariably be offered tea as part of the bargaining process. Accepting places you under no obligation to buy. It does, however, allow the seller more time to draw your attention to other potential sales. If you aren't that interested in what he has to offer in the first place, then definitely decline the tea.

The sales pitches of the souk traders are nothing if not amusing. But if you are not interested then just walk on, don't respond and don't catch anybody's eye. No seller is going to waste time on somebody who is not going to purchase goods.

As a rule of thumb, when tempted in the souk always consider how it will look at home. How well will a brass platter the size of a tractor wheel fit with your furniture at home? And would you actually dare to wear the canary-yellow slippers and take a stroll down a high street at home?

If you want a break from the always busy souks and wish to purchase something unique but distinctly Moroccan, visit some of the shops that line the Medina.

Where to Eat

Broadly speaking, there are two types of restaurant in Marrakech: those that offer Moroccan food and those that offer international food. The Moroccan restaurants either feature an à la carte or set menu. Set-menu meals consist of a starter (soup or salad), followed by a main dish and finishing with a dessert (usually something like a crème caramel or fruit). However, at more expensive restaurants such a meal can involve

ridiculous numbers of courses. You may end up paying for a lot more food than you could possibly eat. Tread carefully. If you grow weary of Moroccan cuisine, then head out to the new town, Guéliz, where you will find a greater variety of international restaurants.

Tipping

You are expected to tip in restaurants and cafés. As a rule of thumb, leave about 10 per cent unless a service charge is included. You are also expected to tip porters (about 20 Dh is the usual amount) and the staff at your riad – leave 100 Dh on top of the bill.

Where to Stay

Marrakech has an abundance of stylish accommodation, much of which comprises either riads or maisons d'hôtes, a term that roughly translates as "boutique hotels".

A riad (the word originates from the Arabic for "garden") is a house in the Medina with a courtyard. Uniquely Moroccan, they can range from a cozy four rooms to close to 20, from humble to ultra-stylish. Nearly all are privately owned guesthouses and the levels of service and luxury tend to reflect the personalities – and financial resources – of their owners. It is usually possible to rent a whole riad at a reduced rate. Many riads offer transport to and from the airport: ask about this when making your booking.

All the riads are in the Medina. The closer you are to Jemaa el Fna, the central whirlpool of Marrakech, the better. The big international hotels are in Hivernage, between the Medina and the airport – a taxi ride away from all the action. There is also a clutch of super-exclusive luxury hideaways and resorts in the Palmeraie.

High season is Christmas and New Year and the weeks around Easter. At such times, prices of rooms can go up by as much as 25 per cent, and that's if you can find one – you really need to have something booked months in advance. September and October are generally also busy as the worst of the summer heat is over. January and February are low season.

Negotiating a lower price for a hotel room is common, and fruitful. At times, it can be possible to obtain reductions of up to 30 per cent. It is a waste of time, however, during the high season.

DIRECTORY

SOURCES OF INFORMATION

Office National Marocain du Tourisme
Open 9am–noon, 3–4:30pm Mon–Fri
📞 0524 43 61 31
🌐 visitmorocco.com

TOURS AND GUIDES

ALSA
🌐 alsa.ma

Travel Link
🌐 travellink.ma
📞 0524 42 48 80

Marrakech Guided Tours
🌐 marrakechguidedtours.wixsite.com

Places to Stay

PRICE CATEGORIES
For a standard, double room per night (with breakfast if included), taxes and extra charges.

Ⓓ under 1,200 Dh   Ⓓ Ⓓ 1,200–2,500 Dh
Ⓓ Ⓓ Ⓓ over 2,500 Dh

Luxury Riads and Hotels

El Fenn
MAP J3 ▪ Derb Moulay Abdallah Ben Hezzian, Medina ▪ 0524 44 12 10 ▪ www.el-fenn.com ▪ Ⓓ Ⓓ Ⓓ
Vanessa Branson's A-list riad features stylish suites and private riads sharing four courtyards, a *hammam*, boutique, library, bar and restaurant, three pools and a screening room.

La Maison Arabe
MAP H2 ▪ 1 derb Assehbé, Medina ▪ 0524 38 70 10 ▪ www.lamaisonarabe. com ▪ Ⓓ Ⓓ Ⓓ
The first riad hotel in Morocco remains one of the best. Owned by Prince Fabrizio Ruspoli, it has 26 ornate rooms mixing traditional Moroccan decor with European old world charm. Amenities include a fine restaurant, pool, spa and affiliated country club.

La Mamounia
MAP H5 ▪ Ave Bab Jedid, Medina ▪ 0524 38 86 00 ▪ www.mamounia.com ▪ Ⓓ Ⓓ Ⓓ
A multimillion-dollar renovation reconfirmed the historic La Mamounia's status as arguably the best and most glamorous hotel in North Africa.

Smartly dressed non-guests may catch a glimpse of the sumptuous interiors by visiting one of the many restaurants or bars *(see pp34–5)*.

Riad Enija
MAP K2 ▪ 9 derb Mesfioui, Medina ▪ 0524 44 09 26 ▪ www. riadenija.com ▪ Ⓓ Ⓓ Ⓓ
Three adjoined houses and a wild garden courtyard make up this striking riad. Rooms verge on the fantastical, with furniture fashioned by international artists. Do you photograph or sleep in the beds?

Riad Farnatchi
MAP K2 ▪ 2 derb Farnatchi, Medina ▪ 0524 38 49 10 ▪ www. riadfarnatchi.com ▪ Ⓓ Ⓓ Ⓓ
Five houses were remodelled to create ten suites, two courtyards and numerous beautiful public spaces. Moroccan-meets-European in style, while facilities include a restaurant, spa, *hammam* and complimentary *djellabas* (traditional house robes).

Riad de Tarabel
MAP J2 ▪ 8 derb Sraghna, Medina ▪ 0524 39 17 06 ▪ www.riad-de-tarabel. com ▪ Ⓓ Ⓓ Ⓓ
French owners have brought a touch of Provence to this elegant ten-room riad hidden down a lane by the Dar El Bacha Palace. Delicious lunches and dinners are firmly Moroccan, and the rooftop terrace offers wonderful views of the Medina.

Royal Mansour
MAP G3/4 ▪ rue Abou El Abbas Sebti, Medina ▪ 0529 80 80 80 ▪ www. royalmansour.com ▪ Ⓓ Ⓓ Ⓓ
Service at this top hotel begins at the airport, where guests are met and whisked through customs and chauffeured to this exclusive city-centre retreat of mini villas set in manicured gardens. It is the last word in privacy, opulence and VIP treatment, but then it is owned by the King of Morocco.

La Sultana
MAP K6 ▪ 403 rue de la Kasbah, Medina ▪ 0524 38 80 08 ▪ www. lasultanahotels.com ▪ Ⓓ Ⓓ Ⓓ
This luxury hotel is discreetly hidden off a courtyard beside the Saadian Tombs. The interiors, a riot of Asian and African styles, are a complete contrast. It's one of the few hotels in the Medina with a decent-sized pool (plus spa).

Villa des Orangers
MAP J5 ▪ 6 rue Sidi Mimoun, Medina ▪ 0524 38 46 38 ▪ www. villadesorangers.com ▪ Ⓓ Ⓓ Ⓓ
A grand residence that once belonged to a judge, this boutique hotel has 27 suites arranged around two beautiful courtyards.

The lovely roof terrace has unrivalled views of the Koutoubia.

International Hotels

Ibis Marrakech Centre Gare
MAP B5 ■ Ave Hassan II, Guéliz ■ 0525 07 25 27 ■ www.ibis.com ⊚
A standard Ibis hotel, with 109 air-conditioned, basic but comfortable rooms. There is a garden and pool. The hotel is close to the train station and the long-distance bus station.

Bab Hotel
MAP B5 ■ Cnr blvd Mansour Eddahbi and rue Mohammed El Beqqal, Guéliz ■ 0524 43 52 50 ■ babhotel marrakech.ma/en/ ■ ⊚ ⊚
A stylish, modern boutique hotel in the New City. Rooms are white and minimalist, kitted out with flatscreen TVs, desks and Nespresso machines. There's a buzzing rooftop bar and ground-floor restaurant. You could be in Madrid or Milan.

Les Jardins de la Koutoubia
MAP J3 ■ 26 rue de la Koutoubia, Medina ■ 0524 38 88 00 ■ www. lesjardinsdelakoutoubia. com ⊚ ⊚
Steps away from the Koutoubia, this well-concealed five-star hotel is relatively modern. The rooms are smart and have full facilities. A swimming pool dominates the central courtyard, while the roof garden has lovely views of the mosque.

Le Méridien N'Fis
MAP C7 ■ Ave Mohammed VI, Hivernage ■ 0524 33 94 00 ■ www.lemeridien nfis.com ■ ⊚ ⊚
A five-minute taxi ride from the Medina. It has 277 rooms, restaurants, a popular nightclub and an excellent spa. The architecture is utilitarian but it does have a nice garden setting.

Radisson Blu
MAP C5 ■ 166–176 ave Mohammed V, Guéliz ■ 0525 07 70 00 ■ www. radissonblu.com ■ ⊚ ⊚
Opened in 2016, this hotel is a competitively priced five-star attached to the new Carré Eden shopping complex. The hotel has 198 contemporary, high-spec rooms and is a 20-minute walk from the Medina but still central to the shops, restaurants, bars and entertainment of the New City.

Royal Mirage Marrakech
MAP C7 ■ Ave de la Menara, Hivernage ■ 0524 35 10 00 ■ www. royalmiragehotels.com ■ ⊚ ⊚
In this former Sheraton property set within its own walled gardens, 661 rooms are laid out around a vast pool. Other amenities include a spa as well as six restaurants and bars.

Savoy Le Grand
MAP C6 ■ Ave Prince Moulay Rachid, Hivernage ■ 0524 35 10 00 ■ www. savoylegrandhotel marrakech.com ■ ⊚ ⊚
A 15-minute walk from the Medina, this is a large, modern, resort-style

hotel with wings arcing around a large central swimming pool. It's attractive, well-maintained and a very good deal for the price.

Sofitel Marrakech
MAP C6 ■ Rue Harroun Errachid, Hivernage ■ 0524 42 56 00 ■ www. sofitel.com ■ ⊚ ⊚
An extremely attractive 207-room property with Moroccan architecture, large, bright rooms and a location right on the doorstep of the Medina. What's more, the excellent Comptoir Darna (see p83) and Table du Marché restaurants are just across the road.

Four Seasons
MAP B6 ■ 1 blvd de la Menara, Hivernage ■ 0524 35 92 00 ■ www. fourseasons.com/ marrakech ■ ⊚ ⊚ ⊚
Opened in 2011, the property lies between the Medina and airport, close to the Menara Gardens. It takes the form of a cluster of low-lying rose-coloured buildings set in 16 ha (40 acres) of beautifully landscaped gardens. Service and amenities are top class.

Hotel Es Saadi
MAP C6 ■ Rue Ibrahim El Mazini, Hivernage ■ 0524 33 74 00 ■ www.essaadi. com ■ ⊚ ⊚
The Rolling Stones hung out here in the 1960s but the hotel has moved with the times and still feels contemporary and luxurious. Set in extensive gardens, it offers 150 rooms and 90 suites, plus ten villas with private pool. There is also a serene spa.

Mid-Range Riads

Dar Attajmil

MAP J3 ▪ 23 rue Laksour, off rue Sidi El Yamami ▪ 0524 42 69 66 ▪ www.darattajmil.com ▪ (Dh)

A lovely little riad with just four rooms. It's a short meandering walk north of Jemaa el Fna, and convenient for exploring the souks and Mouassine neighbourhood. This is an intimate, friendly place that bears the stamp of its (English-speaking) Italian owner.

Dar Doukkala

MAP H2 ▪ 83 rue Bab Doukkala, Bab El Bacha ▪ 0524 38 34 44 ▪ www.dardoukkala.com ▪ (Dh)

Seven rooms and suites in this enchanting *maison d'hôtes* are filled with wonderful period details. Other eccentricities include a wall of lanterns above a small terrace pool. The two suites have private terraces.

Les Jardins de la Medina

MAP K7 ▪ 21 derb Chtouka, Quartier Kasbah ▪ 0524 38 18 51 ▪ www.lesjardinsdelamedina.com ▪ (Dh)(Dh)

It is not hard to see why a 19th-century prince chose this riad for his residence. Set in luxuriant gardens, this chic establishment has 36 rooms that blend modern amenities with traditional Moroccan splendour. There is also a lovely pool, a *hammam* and a respected Moroccan cookery school.

Riad 72

MAP H2 ▪ 72 Arset Awsel, Bab Doukkala ▪ 0524 38 76 29 ▪ www.riad72.com ▪ (Dh)(Dh)

This stylish, Italian-owned riad is very Milan-meets-Marrakech. The house is traditional but the furniture is all imported. There is one dramatically large main suite, a small suite and five double rooms, plus a solarium and a *hammam*.

Riad Adore

MAP J2 ▪ 94 derb Tizouagrine, Dar El Bacha ▪ 0524 37 77 37 ▪ www.riadadore.com ▪ (Dh)(Dh)

A beautiful ten-room riad created by a French architect, so it's no surprise it's a real looker. It has a spa, swimming pool and library, as well as lovely roof terraces and salons. The location is excellent, right in the thick of the souks.

Riad AnaYela

MAP J1 ▪ 28 derb Zerwal, Bab El Khemis ▪ 0524 38 69 69 ▪ www.anayela.de ▪ (Dh)(Dh)

A 300-year-old house renovated by a German entrepreneur, who has created something quite magical in this far north corner of the Medina. With only five rooms, it feels like a secret retreat, with a grand indoor courtyard with heated pool, and a spacious rooftop terrace.

Riad Kheirredine

MAP H1 ▪ 2 derb Chelligui, Sidi Ben Slimane ▪ 0524 38 63 64 ▪ www.riadkheirredine.com ▪ (Dh)(Dh)

Hidden away up in the north of the Medina, this Italian-managed three-storey riad has

11 gorgeously decorated deluxe rooms and suites. There are two pools, a *hammam* and a spa.

Riad Kniza

MAP G1 ▪ 34 derb L'Hôtel, Bab Doukkala ▪ 0524 37 69 42 ▪ www.riadkniza.com ▪ (Dh)(Dh)

A palatial riad filled with objets d'art. For 35 years its Moroccan antique dealer/owner has been the go-to guide to the city for celebrities, showing around stars such as Tom Cruise and Brad Pitt, and at least one US president.

Riad Al Massarah

MAP H1 ▪ 26 derb Jdid, Bab Doukkala ▪ 0524 38 32 06 ▪ www.riadalmassarah.com ▪ (Dh)(Dh)

A bright, six-room riad with rooms on the first floor overlooking a central courtyard with turquoise plunge pool. There's also a dining room, *hammam*, massage room and library. It has won awards for its environmental and employee welfare policies.

Riad El Mezouar

MAP L3 ▪ 28 derb El Hammam ▪ 0524 38 09 49 ▪ www.mezouar.com ▪ (Dh)(Dh)

A serene, whitewashed riad with a courtyard pool and large rooms fitted with lovely traditional furnishings. Its only slight drawback is the location – a 15-minute walk from Jemaa el Fna.

Riyad Al Moussika

MAP K3 ▪ 62 derb Boutouil, Kennaria ▪ 0524 38 90 67 ▪ www.riyad-al-moussika.com ▪ (Dh)(Dh)

A beautifully restored and maintained former grandee's home, Al

Moussika is especially notable for its good food – including an enormous breakfast spread of eggs, pancakes, pastries and fruit. The *hammam*, pool and roof terrace complete the package.

Riad Noga
MAP L3 ▪ 78 derb Jdid, Douar Graoua ▪ 0524 38 52 46 ▪ www.riadnoga. com ▪ (Dh) (Dh)
A spacious German-run riad with a homely air and efficient service, it has seven rooms, three roof terraces and a decent-sized pool, and all the rooms come with TV sets, sound systems and cosy fireplaces for cool nights.

Riad l'Orangeraie
MAP J2 ▪ 61 rue Sidi El Yamani, Mouassine ▪ 0661 23 87 89 ▪ www. riadorangeraie.com ▪ (Dh) (Dh)
Created by two French brothers, this riad has seven comfortable rooms set around two courtyards, one of which is planted, the other filled by a sparkling plunge pool. The location is excellent, in the heart of buzzing Mouassine.

Riad Les Yeux Bleus
MAP H2 ▪ 7 derb El Ferrane, Bab Doukkala ▪ 0524 37 81 61 ▪ www. marrakesh-boutique-riad. com ▪ (Dh) (Dh)
Despite the name, the eight beautifully designed guestrooms here are painted various vivid tones of blue, yellow and green. It makes for cheerful surroundings, aided by super-friendly staff and good amenities including two pools, a sun terrace and a library.

Talaa 12
MAP K2 ▪ 12 Talaa Ben Youssef ▪ 0524 42 90 45 ▪ www.talaa12.com ▪ (Dh) (Dh)
This contemporary, eight-room riad decorated in a simple and unclut-tered, yet appealing style. The traditional feel that permeates the place is augmented by modern comforts such as air conditioning and a *hammam*. It is located right on the doorstep of the souks.

Riad Noir d'Ivoire
MAP K3 ▪ 31–33 derb Jdid, Bab Doukkala ▪ 0524 38 09 75 ▪ www. noir-d-ivoire.com ▪ (Dh) (Dh) (Dh)
In terms of decor, this is something else: a playful and eccentric take on modern Moroccan. Combine two courtyards with plunge pools, a gym, spa, boutique, restaurant with wine cellar, as well as a dinky cocktail bar for one of the hippest places to stay in town.

Budget Riads and Hostels

Chambres d'Amis
MAP K3 ▪ 46/47 derb Moulay Abdelkader, off derb Dabachi, Medina ▪ 0524 42 69 65 ▪ www. chambresdamis.com ▪ (Dh)
A beautiful feminine riad owned and fashioned by Dutch interior designer Anke van der Pluijm. The six guestrooms are lively with colourful kitsch and craftwork, and there's a courtyard garden and roof terrace. Staff can organise cookery and crochet classes, and even bird-watching outings.

Djemaa El Fna Hotel Cecil
MAP J3 ▪ Derb Sidi Bouloukate, Medina ▪ 0662 06 11 76 ▪ www. djemaaelfnahotelcecil. org ▪ (Dh)
This hostel-like hotel offers good value for money, given its central location and facilities, which include en-suite rooms, a rooftop terrace and Wi-Fi.

Hotel Ali
MAP J4 ▪ Rue Moulay Ismail, Medina ▪ 0524 44 49 79 ▪ www.hotel-ali.com ▪ No credit cards ▪ (Dh)
A popular launch pad for trips to the Atlas Mountains, this is one of the busiest budget hotels in town. The rooms are a bit of a mixed bag, so inspect a few prior to making your final choice.

Hotel Farouk
MAP B5 ▪ 66 ave Hassan II, Guéliz ▪ 0524 43 19 89 ▪ www.hotelfarouk.com ▪ (Dh)
Owned by the same people as the Hotel Ali, this is one of the best budget options for anyone looking to stay close to the New City. Rooms vary greatly, so check out a few before choosing. All of the rooms are en-suite.

Hotel Le Gallia
MAP J4 ▪ 30 rue de la Recette, off rue de Bab Agnaou, Medina ▪ 0524 44 59 13 ▪ www. hotellegallia.com ▪ (Dh)
Of all the budget options in the bylanes off rue de Bab Agnaou, this is one of the best, with en-suite rooms arranged around two Andalusian-style courtyards. Be sure to book in advance.

For a key to hotel price categories see p112

Hotel Medina

MAP K4 ■ 1 derb Sidi
Bouloukat, Medina
■ 0524 44 29 97
■ www.hotelmedina
marrakech.com ■ (Dh)
On a street full of cheap
rooms, Hotel Medina stands
out for its relative clean-
liness and the hospitality
of the owners. The really
impecunious can sleep on
the roof terrace for just 30
Dh. Note that the showers
here are communal.

Hotel Sherazade

MAP K4 ■ 3 derb Djama,
Medina ■ 0524 42 93 05
■ www.hotelsherazade.
com ■ (Dh)
This hotel offers a wide
range of rooms, from
mini-apartments to simple
rooms with shared bath-
rooms. It has a lovely tiled
courtyard and an extensive
roof terrace with a tent
area for dining. Beds in
shared rooms start at
under 200 Dh.

Hotel du Trésor

MAP J3 ■ 7 Sidi Bouloukat,
off Riad Zitoun Kedim,
Medina ■ 0524 37 51 13
■ www.hotel-du-tresor.
hotelsmarrakech.net
■ No credit cards ■ (Dh)
Close to the main square,
this little gem of a hotel.
It has been around since
the early 1950s and its 14
guestrooms, plunge pool
and salon retain a retro feel.
You could imagine Paul
Bowles (see p42) hanging
out in the salon here.

Les Jardins de Mouassine

MAP J3 ■ 20 derb Chorfa
El Kebir, Mouassine,
Medina ■ 0672 58 10 78
■ www.lesjardinsde
mouassine.com ■ (Dh)
This hotel offers some of
the style and charm of the

more expensive riads but
with the option of competitively priced, hotel-style
double rooms. Facilities
include a library, bar,
plunge pool, *hammam*
and a barbecue grill on
the terrace. Cots are also
available on request.

Riad Altair

MAP H2 ■ 21 derb Zaouia,
Bab Doukkala, Medina
■ 0524 38 52 24 ■ www.
riadaltair.com ■ (Dh)
Close to the Bab Doukkala
mosque, this is an intimate
little riad with six elegant
rooms, a games room and
library. While there is no
restaurant, there is a
kitchen and meals can
be taken al fresco on the
pleasant roof terrace.

Riad Berbère

MAP K2 ■ 23 derb Sidi
Ahmed Ben Nasser, off
Kaat Benahid, Medina
■ 0524 38 19 10 ■ www.
leriadberbere.com ■ (Dh)
A beautiful, light-filled
17th-century riad,
sensitively renovated in
an elegant, minimalist style.
It has a lovely planted
central courtyard with
ornamental swimming
pool. There is a small
hammam and staff can
organize cooking lessons,
yoga sessions and day
trips out of town. Cheaper
rooms are available.

Riad Al Jazira

MAP D4 ■ 8 derb Mayara,
Sidi Ben Sliman, Medina
■ 0524 42 64 63 ■ www.
riad-aljazira.com ■ (Dh)
One of several properties
owned and operated by
Marrakech Riads, which
is run by Abdellatif Aït
Ben Abdallah, who was
partly responsible for
the city's 20th-century
renaissance. Three

houses knocked into one,
it's a large property with a
good-size pool in the main
courtyard and a lovely roof
terrace. It's in a quieter
part of the Medina, which
could be a positive or a
negative depending on
your holiday outlook.

Riad Jnane Mogador

MAP K4 ■ 116 rue Riad
Zitoun El Kedim, derb
Sidi Bouloukat, Medina
■ 0524 42 63 23 ■ www.
jnanemogador.com ■ (Dh)
A restored 19th-century
residence that falls
between a riad and hotel,
it has 17 rooms around
a central courtyard with a
fountain and grand stair-
case. The decor may lack
sophistication, but it also
has a spa and is good
value for money.

Riad Nejma Lounge

MAP G1 ■ 45 derb Sidi
M'hamed El Haj, Bab
Doukkala ■ 0644 48 57 87
■ www.riadnejmalounge.
com ■ (Dh)
With six rooms decked
out in striking colours,
this is one of the funkiest
riads in town. A plunge
pool in the courtyard and
a roof terrace add to its
"loungey" feel.

Riad Tizwa

MAP J2 ■ 26 derb El
Guerraba, Riad Laarous,
Medina ■ 07973 115 471
(UK) or 310 854 2834 (US)
■ www.riadtizwa.com
■ (Dh)
A cool, laid-back and fun
English-run riad with
a great location in the
souks, the Tizwa has six
rooms on three floors.
There's a small *hammam*,
and a pleasant roof
terrace for catching the
sun, reading books and
al fresco dining.

Tchaikana
MAP K2 ■ 25 derb El
Ferrane, Quartier Azbezt,
Medina ■ 0524 38 51 50
■ www.tchaikana.com
■ (Dh) (Dh)
Close to the Musée de
Marrakech, this riad has
two suites, two big double
rooms, and one smaller
double room. Delphine,
one half of the friendly
Belgian couple who run
the place, is an expert in
souk shopping. Cheaper
rooms are available.

The Palmeraie and Further Afield

Caravanserai
264 Ouled Ben Rahmoune,
40,000 ■ 0524 30 03 02
■ www.caravanserai.ma
■ (Dh)
A conversion of several
village dwellings north of
Marrakech, this hotel
offers a stunning mud-
brick architecture as well
as suites with their own
pool. There are also lots
of terraces and a *hammam*.

Les Deux Tours
Douar Abiad, Palmeraie
■ 0524 25 26 27 ■ www.
les-deux-tours.com
■ (Dh) (Dh)
A landmark piece of
architecture by Charles
Boccara, this is a beautiful
walled retreat of inter-
connected villas set in
lush Andalusian-style
gardens with pools and
fountains. The softly
seductive rooms make
lavish use of Boccara's
trademark *tadelakt*.

Fairmont Royal Palm
Km 12, route d'Amizmiz
■ 0524 48 78 00 ■ www.
fairmont.com/marrakech
■ (Dh) (Dh)
Covering 231 hectares
(571 acres) of orange,

palm and olive trees,
this hotel, located 20
minutes south of the
city centre, will have
strong appeal to two
groups: spa fanatics
and golfers. The former
are catered for with an
enormous spa, the latter
by the Royal Palm
Golf Club.

Palmeraie Palace
Circuit de la Palmeraie
■ 0524 33 43 43 ■ www.
palmeraieresorts.com
■ (Dh) (Dh)
This large five-star hotel
on the northern edge
of the Palmeraie, with
a golf course attached,
also has pools, gardens,
tennis courts, restaurants
and a popular nightclub.

Amanjena
Km 12, route de
Ouarzazate ■ 0524 39 90
00 ■ www.aman.com
■ (Dh) (Dh) (Dh)
Part of the ultra-exclusive
Amanresorts group,
the place resembles a
film set of an Arabian
epic – appropriate given
the number of film
stars and other A-listers
that check in here.
Accommodation consists
of 39 private villas,
some with their own
walled gardens.

Jnane Tamsna
Douar Abiad, Palmeraie
■ 0524 32 84 84
■ www.jnanetamsna.com
■ (Dh) (Dh) (Dh)
This coolest and most
elegant of the Palmeraie
villas has featured in
magazines but there's
plenty of substance
here too – surrounding
fruit orchards, and
vegetable and herb
gardens provide the
all-organic produce for

the kitchen. Cheaper
rooms are available.

Ksar Char-Bagh
Jnane Abiad, Palmeraie
■ 0524 32 92 44 ■ www.
ksarcharbagh.com
■ (Dh) (Dh) (Dh)
This mad Marrakech
hotel is a re-creation
of an Alhambran palace
court on a grand scale.
It's all about excess –
from the heated pool
to the cigar salon. The
hotel will pick up guests
from the airport in old
London taxis.

Mandarin Oriental
Route du Golf Royal
■ 0524 29 88 88 ■ www.
mandarinoriental.com/
marrakech ■ (Dh) (Dh) (Dh)
Opened in 2015, the
Mandarin has 54 single-
storey villas, all with
private pools, in a
beautiful garden ten-
minutes' drive southeast
of the Medina. Expect top-
class facilities including
three restaurants, indoor
and outdoor swimming
pools, a spa and access to
two golf courses.

Palais Namaskar
Route de Bab Atlas,
Palmeraie ■ 0524 29
98 00 ■ www.palais
namaskar.com ■ (Dh) (Dh) (Dh)
The Namaskar is a grand
property located 20
minutes northeast of the
Medina in the Palmeraie.
It combines grand
architecture and vistas
with landscaped grounds,
super-spacious rooms
and suites, and a full-
service spa as well as
yoga and fitness centres.
If you are not a guest, it
is worth visiting just for
the rooftop No Mad Bar
with its views of the
Atlas Mountains.

For a key to hotel price categories see p112

General Index

Acknowledgments

Author

Andrew Humphreys is a London-based journalist and writer with a particular passion for the Middle East and North Africa. He has written extensively on Morocco for a variety of newspapers, magazines and publishing companies, and is a frequent visitor to Marrakech.

Publishing Director Georgina Dee

Publisher Vivien Antwi

Design Director Phil Ormerod

Editorial Ankita Awasthi Tröger, Rachel Fox, Maresa Manara, Freddie Marriage, Sally Schafer, Penny Walker

Revisions Lucy Sienkowska, Akanksha Siwach, Priyanka Thakur

Commissioned Photography Alan Keohane

Design Tessa Bindloss, Bharti Karakoti, Marisa Renzullo, Ankita Sharma, Stuti Tiwari Bhatia

Jacket Design Richard Czapnik

Picture Research Taiyaba Khatoon, Ellen Root, Rituraj Singh

Cartography Zafar ul Islam Khan, Suresh Kumar, James Macdonald, Casper Morris

DTP Jason Little

Production Jude Crozier

Factchecker Mary Novakovich

Proofreader Kathryn Glendenning

Indexer Helen Peters

Picture Credits

The publisher would like to thank the following for their kind permission to reproduce their photographs:
Key: a-above; b-below/bottom; c-centre; f-far; l-left; r-right; t-top

123RF.com: Tudor Antonel Adrian 11crb; Birgit Korber 32bc; Pulpitis 19br; Oleg Seleznev 16-7.

33 rue Majorelle: 82cla.

4Corners: SIME/Paolo Giocoso 14-5.

Alamy Stock Photo: AA World Travel Library 27tc, 79br, 80tl; AF archive 34bl; Africa 79t; AGE Fotostock 99br; Bon Appetit 58br; Paul Carstairs 88cb; Dbimages 96cb; PE Forsberg 96tr; Kevin Foy 17tl, 52tr; FreeProd 18t; Adam Goodwin 10cla, 13br; Granger Historical Picture Archive 42bl; Grant Rooney Premium 14clb; Rosemary Harris 25br; Hemis 1, 3tr, 52clb, 53cra, 68cla, 76cb, 104-5; Idealink Photography 53b; imageBROKER 11cl, 35tr;

Images & Stories 70t; Franck Jeannin 84-5; Shirley Kilpatrick 13br; Art Kowalsky 67b; Karol Kozlowski 4t; Alistair Laming 10br; Chris Lawrence 27crb; Mark Lees 78tl; LOOK Die Bildagentur der Fotografen GmbH 47br; Rob Matthews 20cla; Eric Nathan 20bc; Efrain Padro 11tr; Olga Popkova 59tr; Quantum Pictures 22-3, 66cla; Robertharding 2tl, 3tl, 8-9, 35crb, 64-5; Grant Rooney 54t, 93br; Shoults 38cla; Dave Stamboulis 87bl; Paul Strawson 86cla; Paul Street 26clb; Kevin Su 100tr; Sebastian Wasek 31br; Tim E White 56clb, 76cla; Jan Wlodarczyk 4crb, 50tl, 88t; Andrew Woodley 30cl; Patrizia Wyss 13tl.

AWL Images: Mauricio Abreu 58tl.

Dar Al Hossoun: Dominique Larosière 51crb.

Dar Daïf: 103cr.

David Bloch Gallery: 40tl.

Dreamstime.com: Tudor Antonel Adrian 80b; Dbajurin 4b; Devy 12cl; Rene Drouyer 11c; Flavijus 19tr; Freeshot 24-5; Abdul Sami Haqqani 25tl; Jahmaican 21tr; Javarman 10cl; Thomas Jurkowski 7cr; Kemaltaner 4cl; Sergii Koval 59cl; Karol Kozlowski 50b, 62tr, 75cl; Madrugaverde 10cr; Masar1920 20-1; Giuseppe Masci 32-3; Mbasil 6cla; Paweł Opaska 12br, 102cla; Piotr Pawinski 4clb; Pipa100 29tl; Andrea Poole 81cla; Ppy2010ha 59bc; Sspezi 17bl; Bidouze Stéphane 29bl; Simon Thomas 18cb; Anibal Trejo 28-9, 30br, 31clb; Sergii Velychko 30-1; Witr 99t; Yakthai 10bl.

Dunes & Desert: 55br.

Getty Images: Mauricio Abreu 26br; Glen Allison 92tl; Bettmann 43cla; Charles Bowman 89clb; Bartosz Hadyniak 93t; Simeone Huber 101cl; Hulton Archive / H. F. Davis 35c; Ipsumpix 38b; Nadia Isakova 98tl, 100b; The John Deakin Archive 39tr; Kelly Cheng Travel Photography 74br; Jason Kempin 41br; Izzet Keribar 74t; Jean-Pierre Lescourret 44tr, 61crb; Lonely Planet 46bl, 54bc; 72cla; Movie Poster Image Art 43br; Martin Moxter 26-7; Conde Nast Collection / Patrick Lichfield 42cr; Laurie Noble 73tr; Richard T. Nowitz 28clb, 44b; Sergio Pitamitz 15tl; Massimo Pizzotti 68b; Paul Quayle 15crb; Reporters Associes 39cl; Robertharding / Matthew Williams-Ellis 32cl; Abdelhak Senna 33tl; Paul A. Souders 12c; Mark Thomas 29crb; Yvan Travert 87tr.

Hotel Villa Maroc: 90t.

iStockphoto.com: Fafou 24clb; FrankvandenBergh 45tr; GuyBerresfordPhotography 19clb; Bartosz Hadyniak 102b; Lukasz Janyst 7tr; javarman3 45cl; Sylwia Kania 94-5; Zdenek Last 58c;

Elzbieta Sekowska 33cr.

Kasbah du Toubkal (www.kasbahdutoubkal. com): Alan Keohane 63b.

Kasbah Tamadot: 97br.

Kechmara: 83br.

La Maison Arabe: 49crb.

La Mamounia: 11bl, 34-5, 35bl, 67cra.

La Sultana Hotels: 47t.

Le Foundouk: 60tl, 77crb.

Maison de la Photographie: 41tl.

Maison Tiskiwin: 69tl.

Marrakech Biennale: 40crb.

Nikki Beach: 57b.

Nomad: 60b.

Oasiria: 55cl.

Pepe Nero: 71cr.

Photoshot: PYMCA 57tr; Retna Pictures / Starface 42tl.

Riad Farnatchi: 48br.

Riad Kniza: 2tr, 4cr, 36-7, 48t.

Robert Harding Picture Library: Stefan Auth 4cla; Ethel Davies 94tl; Lee Frost 16clb; Christian Kober 63tr.

Taros: 91br.

Cover

Front and spine: **Getty Images:** Thanachai Wachiraworakam

Back: **Dreamstime.com:** Danmir12

Pull Out Map Cover

Getty Images: Thanachai Wachiraworakam

All other images © Dorling Kindersley

For further information see:
www.dkimages.com

Penguin
Random
House

Printed and bound in China

First First American Edition, 2008
Published in the US by
DK Publishing, 345 Hudson Street,
New York, New York 10014

Copyright 2008, 2018 © Dorling
Kindersley Limited

A Penguin Random House Company

18 19 20 10 9 8 7 6 5 4 3 2 1

**Reprinted with revisions 2010, 2012,
2014, 2018**

Published in Great Britain by Dorling Kindersley Limited.

A catalog record for this book is available from the Library of Congress.

ISSN 1479-344X
ISBN 978 1 4654 6062 2

MIX
Paper from
responsible sources
FSC™ C018179

SPECIAL EDITIONS OF DK TRAVEL GUIDES

DK Travel Guides can be purchased in bulk quantities at discounted prices for use in promotions or as premiums. We are also able to offer special editions and personalized jackets, corporate imprints, and excerpts from all of our books, tailored specifically to meet your own needs.

To find out more, please contact:

in the US
specialsales@dk.com

in the UK
travelguides@uk.dk.com

in Canada
specialmarkets@dk.com

in Australia
**penguincorporatesales@
penguinrandomhouse.com.au**

As a guide to abbreviations in visitor information blocks: **Adm** = admission charge; **D** = dinner; **L** = lunch.

Phrase Book: French

In Emergency

Help!	**Au secours!**	oh sekoor
Stop!	**Arrêtez!**	aret-ay
Call a doctor!	**Appelez un médecin!**	apuh-lay uñ medsañ
Call an ambulance!	**Appelez une ambulance!**	apuh-lay oon oñboo-loñs
Call the police!	**Appelez la police!**	apuh-lay lah poh-lees
Call the fire brigade!	**Appelez les pompiers!**	apuh-lay leh poñ-peeyay

Communication Essentials

Yes/No	**Oui/Non**	wee/noñ
Please	**S'il vous plaît**	seel voo play
Thank you	**Merci**	mer-see
Excuse me	**Excusez-moi**	exkoo-zay mwah
Hello	**Bonjour**	boñzhoor
Goodbye	**Au revoir**	oh ruh-vwar
Good evening	**Bonsoir**	boñ-swar
What?	**Quoi?**	kwah
When?	**Quand?**	koñ
Why?	**Pourquoi?**	poor-kwah
Where?	**Où?**	oo

Useful Phrases

How are you?	**Comment allez-vous?**	kom-moñ talay voo
Very well,	**Très bien**	treh byañ
Pleased to meet you.	**Enchanté**	oñshoñ-tay
Where is/are…?	**Où est/sont…?**	oo ay/soñ
Which way to…?	**Quelle est la direction pour…?**	kel ay lah deer-ek-syoñ poor
Do you speak English?	**Parlez-vous anglais?**	par-lay voo oñg-lay
I don't understand.	**Je ne comprends pas.**	zhuh nuh kom-proñ pah
I'm sorry.	**Excusez-moi.**	exkoo-zay mwah

Useful Words

big	**grand**	groñ
small	**petit**	puh-tee
hot	**chaud**	show
cold	**froid**	frwah
good	**bon**	boñ
bad	**mauvais**	moh-veh
open	**ouvert**	oo-ver
closed	**fermé**	fer-meh
left	**gauche**	gohsh
right	**droite**	drwaht
entrance	**l'entrée**	l'on-tray
exit	**la sortie**	sor-tee
toilet	**les toilettes**	twah-let

Shopping

How much does this cost?	**C'est combien s'il vous plaît?**	say kom-byañ seel voo play
I would like …	**Je voudrais…**	zhuh voo-dray
Do you have?	**Est-ce que vous avez?**	es-kuh voo zavay
Do you take credit cards?	**Est-ce que vous acceptez les cartes de crédit?**	es-kuh voo zaksept-ay leh kart duh kreh-dee

What time do you open?	**A quelle heure êtes-vous ouvert?**	ah kel urr et voo oo-ver
What time do you close?	**A quelle heure êtes-vous fermé?**	ah kel urr et voo fer-may
This one.	**Celui-ci.**	suhl-wee-see
That one.	**Celui-là.**	suhl-wee-lah
expensive	**cher**	shehr
cheap	**pas cher, bon marché**	pah shehr, boñ mar-shay
size, clothes	**la taille**	tye
size, shoes	**la pointure**	pwañ-tur
white	**blanc**	bloñ
black	**noir**	nwahr
red	**rouge**	roozh
yellow	**jaune**	zhohwn
green	**vert**	vehr
blue	**bleu**	bluh

Types of Shop

antique shop	**le magasin d'antiquités**	maga-zañ d'oñteekee-tay
bakery	**la boulangerie**	booloñ-zhuree
bank	**la banque**	boñk
bookshop	**la librairie**	lee-brehree
cake shop	**la pâtisserie**	patee-sree
cheese shop	**la fromagerie**	fromazh-ree
chemist	**la pharmacie**	farmah-see
department store	**le grand magasin**	groñ maga-zañ
delicatessen	**l'épicerie**	lay-pee-sree
gift shop	**le magasin de cadeaux**	maga-zañ duh kadoh
greengrocer	**le marchand de légumes**	mar-shoñ duh lay-goom
grocery	**l'alimentation**	alee-moñta-syoñ
market	**le marché**	marsh-ay
newsagent	**le magasin de journaux**	maga-zañ duh zhoor-no
post office	**la poste, le bureau de poste, le PTT**	pohst, booroh duh pohst, peh-teh-teh
supermarket	**le supermarché**	soo pehr-marshay
tobacconist	**le tabac**	tabah
travel agent	**l'agence de voyages**	l'azhoñs duh vwayazh

Sightseeing

art gallery	**la galerie d'art**	galer-ree dart
bus station	**la gare routière**	gahr roo-tee-yehr
church	**l'église**	l'aygleez
garden	**le jardin**	zhar-dañ
library	**la bibliothèque**	beebleeo-tek
mosque	**la mosquée**	mos-qay
museum	**le musée**	moo-zay
railway station	**la gare**	gahr
tourist information office	**renseignements touristiques, le syndicat d'initiative**	roñsayn-moñ toorees-teek, sandee-ka d'eenee-syateev

Staying in a Hotel

Do you have a vacant room?	**Est-ce que vous avez une chambre?**	es-kuh voo-zavay oon shambr
double room, with double bed	**chambre à deux personnes, avec un grand lit**	shambr ah duh pehr-son, avek un groññ lee
twin room	**chambre à deux lits**	shambr ah duh lee

single room	**chambre à une personne**	*shambr ah oon pehr-son*
room with a bath, shower	**chambre avec salle de bains, une douche**	*shambr avek sal duh bañ, oon doosh*
I have a reservation.	**J'ai fait une réservation.**	*zhay fay oon rayzehrva-syoñ*

Eating Out

Have you got a table?	**Avez-vous une table libre?**	*avay-voo oon tahbl duh leebr*
I want to reserve a table.	**Je voudrais réserver une table.**	*zhuh voo-dray rayzehr-vay oon tahbl*
The bill please.	**L'addition s'il vous plaît.**	*l'adee-syoñ seel voo play*
I am a vegetarian.	**Je suis végétarien.**	*zhuh swee vezhay-tehryañ*
waitress/ waiter	**Madame, Mademoiselle/ Monsieur**	*mah-dam, mah-demwahzel/ muh-syuh*
menu	**le menu, la carte**	*men-oo, kart*
fixed-price menu	**le menu à prix fixe**	*men-oo ah pree feeks*
cover charge	**le couvert**	*koo-vehr*
wine list	**la carte des vins**	*kart-deh vañ*
glass	**le verre**	*vehr*
bottle	**la bouteille**	*boo-tay*
knife	**le couteau**	*koo-toh*
fork	**la fourchette**	*for-shet*
spoon	**la cuillère**	*kwee-yehr*
breakfast	**le petit déjeuner**	*puh-tee deh-zhuh-nay*
lunch	**le déjeuner**	*deh-zhuh-nay*
dinner	**le dîner**	*dee-nay*
main course	**le plat principal**	*plah prañsee-pal*
starter, first course	**l'entrée, le hors d'oeuvre**	*l'oñ-tray, or-duhvr*
dish of the day	**le plat du jour**	*plah doo zhoor*
café	**le café**	*ka-fay*

Menu Decoder

baked	**cuit au four**	*kweet oh foor*
beef	**le boeuf**	*buhf*
beer	**la bière**	*bee-yehr*
boiled	**bouilli**	*boo-yee*
bread	**le pain**	*pan*
butter	**le beurre**	*burr*
cake	**le gâteau**	*gah-toh*
cheese	**le fromage**	*from-azh*
chicken	**le poulet**	*poo-lay*
chips	**les frites**	*freet*
chocolate	**le chocolat**	*shoko-lah*
coffee	**le café**	*kah-fay*
dessert	**le dessert**	*deh-ser*
egg	**l'oeuf**	*l'uf*
fish	**le poisson**	*pwah-ssoñ*
fresh fruit	**le fruit frais**	*frwee freh*
garlic	**l'ail**	*l'eye*
grilled	**grillé**	*gree-yay*
ice, ice cream	**la glace**	*glas*
lamb	**l'agneau**	*l'anyoh*
lemon	**le citron**	*see-troñ*
meat	**la viande**	*vee-yand*
milk	**le lait**	*leh*
mineral water	**l'eau minérale**	*l'oh meeney-ral*
oil	**l'huile**	*l'weel*
onions	**les oignons**	*leh zonyoñ*
fresh orange juice	**l'orange pressée**	*l'oroñzh presseh*
fresh lemon juice	**le citron pressé**	*see-troñ presseh*
pepper	**le poivre**	*pwavr*
potatoes	**les pommes de terre**	*pom-duh tehr*
prawns	**les crevettes**	*kruh-vet*
rice	**le riz**	*ree*
roast	**rôti**	*row-tee*
salt	**le sel**	*sel*
sausage	**la saucisse**	*sohsees*
seafood	**les fruits de mer**	*frwee duh mer*
shellfish	**les crustacés**	*kroos-ta-say*
soup	**la soupe, le potage**	*soop, poh-tazh*
steak	**le bifteck, le steack**	*beef-tek, stek*
sugar	**le sucre**	*sookr*
tea	**le thé**	*tay*
vegetables	**les légumes**	*lay-goom*
vinegar	**le vinaigre**	*veenaygr*
water	**l'eau**	*l'oh*
red wine	**le vin rouge**	*vañ roozh*
white wine	**le vin blanc**	*vañ bloñ*

Numbers

0	**zéro**	*zeh-roh*
1	**un, une**	*uñ, oon*
2	**deux**	*duh*
3	**trois**	*trwah*
4	**quatre**	*katr*
5	**cinq**	*sañk*
6	**six**	*sees*
7	**sept**	*set*
8	**huit**	*weet*
9	**neuf**	*nerf*
10	**dix**	*dees*
11	**onze**	*oñz*
12	**douze**	*dooz*
13	**treize**	*trehz*
14	**quatorze**	*katorz*
15	**quinze**	*kañz*
16	**seize**	*sehz*
17	**dix-sept**	*dees-set*
18	**dix-huit**	*dees-weet*
19	**dix-neuf**	*dees-nerf*
20	**vingt**	*vañ*
30	**trente**	*tront*
40	**quarante**	*karoñt*
50	**cinquante**	*sañkoñt*
60	**soixante**	*swasoñt*
70	**soixante-dix**	*swasoñt-dees*
80	**quatre-vingt**	*katr-vañ*
90	**quatre-vingt-dix**	*katr-vañ-dees*
100	**cent**	*soñ*
1,000	**mille**	*meel*

Time

one minute	**une minute**	*oon mee-noot*
one hour	**une heure**	*oon urr*
half an hour	**une demi-heure**	*oon duh-me urr*
one day	**un jour**	*un zhorr*
Monday	**lundi**	*luñ-dee*
Tuesday	**mardi**	*mar-dee*
Wednesday	**mercredi**	*mehrkruh-dee*
Thursday	**jeudi**	*zhuh-dee*
Friday	**vendredi**	*voñdruh-dee*
Saturday	**samedi**	*sam-dee*
Sunday	**dimanche**	*dee-moñsh*

Arabic

Moroccan Arabic is unique to Morocco and is not understood by other Arabic speakers. Moroccans speak faster and abbreviate words. Pronunciation is gentler due to the influence of French.

Useful Words and Phrases

Yes	*Na-am*
No	*Laa*
Hello / Peace be upon you	*Selaam*
Goodbye	*Ma'eel salaama*
Excuse me	*Min fadlak*
Sorry	*Esme'hlee*
Thank you	*Se'hha*
Please	*Min fadlak*
Good morning	*Esbe'h elkheer*
Good evening	*Masaal kheer*
How are you?	*Washraak?*
I'm fine	*Laabas*
I don't understand	*Ana mafhimtaksh*
Do you speak English?	*Tatkalam engleeze-ya?*
God willing	*Inshaala*
big	*kbeer*
small	*sgeer*
hot	*sokhoon*
cold	*baared*
bad	*mashemlee'ha*
good	*mlee'ha*
open	*maftoo'h*
closed	*maghlook*
toilet	*towalett*
a little	*kaleel*
a lot	*bizzaaf*

Emergencies

Stop!	*Owkof!*
Can you call a doctor?	*Momkin kellem el tabeeb?*
Can you call the police?	*Momkin kellem el polees?*

Making a Telephone Call

I'd like to speak to…	*Begheet nekallam…*
This is…	*Hadi…*
Please say… called	*Min fadlak kollo… etkallam*

In a Hotel

Do you have a room?	*Enta 'andak ghorfa?*
With bathroom	*Ma'al 'ham-maam*
single room	*ghorfa le shakhs waa'hid*
double room	*ghorfa le shakhsayn*
shower	*doosh*
key	*meftaa'h*

Shopping

How much is it?	*Kam else'er?*
I'd like…	*Ana 'habbayt*
This one	*Hadi*
That's too much	*Hadi ghaalya*
I'll take it	*Naakhodha*
market	*marshee*
expensive, cheap	*ghaalya, rekheesa*

Sightseeing

art gallery	*galiree daar*
beach	*bhar*
bus station	*stasyon do boos*
entrance	*dokhool*
exit	*khrooj*
garden	*eljonayna*
guide	*geed*
map	*kaart*
mosque	*masjid*
museum	*moozi*

park	*baark*
ticket	*tekee*
tourist office	*mektab soyaa'h*
How much is it to…?	*Kam tekal-laf haazi…?*

Eating Out

Have you got a table for…?	*Enta 'andak towla*
Can I have the bill please?	*Te'eteeni elfatoora min fadlak?*

Menu Decoder

tajeen	steamed pot of vegetables with meat, etc
kuskus	hand-made couscous
elbasteela	pastry filled with vegetables and meat, etc
'hreera	soup
kefta	meatballs with herbs
el'hoot	fish
djaaj	chicken
l'hem	meat
legoom/khodra	vegetables
maa'a	water

Time

today	*el yoom*
yesterday	*el baareh*
tomorrow	*ghadan*
tonight	*felleel*
day	*nehaar*
hour	*sa'aa*
week	*semaana*

Days of the Week

Monday	*el etneen*
Tuesday	*el tlaata*
Wednesday	*el arbe'aa*
Thursday	*el khamees*
Friday	*el jomo'aa*
Saturday	*el sabet*
Sunday	*el a'had*

Numbers

1	*waa'hid*
2	*zooj*
3	*tlaata*
4	*araba'aa*
5	*khamsa*
6	*set-ta*
7	*seba'a*
8	*tmaanya*
9	*tes'aa*
10	*'ashra*
11	*'hdaash*
12	*etnaash*
13	*tlat-taash*
14	*erba'-taash*
15	*khmastaash*
16	*set-taash*
17	*sba'ataash*
18	*tmantaash*
19	*tas'ataash*
20	*eshreen*
21	*waa'hid w'eshreen*
30	*tlatheen*
40	*ereb'een*
50	*khamseen*
60	*set-teen*
70	*seb'een*
80	*tmaneen*
90	*tes'een*
100	*meya*

When you see an apostrophe (') in the Arabic, this means that you pronounce the letter after it with a little puff of air.